JOY IN GRIEF

God's Answer
for Hard Times

DR. JIM HALLA

Ambassador International

GREENVILLE, SOUTH CAROLINA & BELFAST, NORTHERN IRELAND

www.ambassador-international.com

Joy in Grief
God's Answers for Hard Times

Printed in the United States of America

ISBN: 978-1-62020-027-8
eISBN: 978-1-62020-028-5

Cover Design & Page Layout by Matthew Mulder

AMBASSADOR INTERNATIONAL
Emerald House
427 Wade Hampton Blvd.
Greenville, SC 29609, USA
www.ambassador-international.com

AMBASSADOR BOOKS
The Mount
2 Woodstock Link
Belfast, BT6 8DD, Northern Ireland, UK
www.ambassador-international.com

The colophon is a trademark of Ambassador

The grief of it all. Grief — an interesting term. It is a feeling, a response, a mind-set, and it includes thinking and wanting. It is a whole-person activity. Therefore armed with a biblical view of man and the world we live in, we know that the Bible has much to say about grief and grieving. I have been struck by the volumes of information "out there" on the subject. Obviously, people are interested in the subject. As I write in the book, so is God who has much to say about grieving His way. From that perspective alone it behooves us to find out what God does say. That in itself is too mild a statement. God's interest and His teaching must be ours to own and apply.

The book is a clarion call to view change and loss as an opportunity to grieve God's way. The book is intended to help direct you and those God brings into your life to view life in general and change and loss in particular from God's perspective. For some that will require a paradigm shift in thinking and wanting. The book is designed to help you and others to make that shift.

In this book I reference my pamphlet "God's Wisdom for Troubled Times." The pamphlet is a primer designed, in part, more for the "acute" event. The book and pamphlet dovetail each other and my prayer is that you will find them an encouragement and blessing enabling you to grieve God's way or to direct some one in that activity. May God bless as you do.

Contents

Introduction 9

CHAPTER 1
Grief and Grieving 15
CHAPTER 2
The Culture's View of Change, Loss,
and Grief 19
CHAPTER 3
The Christian's Response 25
CHAPTER 4
Jesus, the Believer's Model 39
CHAPTER 5
Application of the Principle of Gain
through Loss 63
CHAPTER 6
The Death of an Unbeliever 71
CHAPTER 7
More Biblical Examples. 75

CHAPTER 8
Objections 85
CHAPTER 9
Conclusion 89
CHAPTER 10
Homework Assignments 95

Appendix A: *lupeo* and *lupe*. *97*
Appendix B: *klaio*. .105
Appendix C: Additional Terms 114
Appendix D: Critique. 117

Introduction

YOU MAY HAVE PICKED UP this book because you have lost someone or something dear to you. As a result of the loss, hurts and thoughts may have come together all at once. Life is so different and seems so complicated now. Your loss may have been sudden and unexpected or slow and anticipated. Either way, its reality weighs heavily. You may be thinking:

- "Just give me time. I'm numb right now."
- "I just don't want to think about it."
- "Why this? Why now? Why me? Why us? What now?"
- "How do I go on? Is there any help? Are there any answers?"
- "Maybe I need a self-help book. Or do I need a counseling program?"
- "Maybe medications and time will help?"
- "I don't think I will ever get over this. I wonder if anything can help me."

Consider these scenarios from the lives of two people perhaps much like you. One is Aunt Joan. She had been married for fifty years and had faithfully gone to church. She was in fair to good health, but suddenly her husband died. She knew he had been sick but not "that sick." His death came as a shock. Now she feels alone. She misses her husband and the many things he did for her. She had told him that he shouldn't die before she did because being alone would be horrible. Now there is no husband—just never-ending details, responsibilities, and obligations, all of which she resents. It becomes obvious to her friends that she is fearful, overwhelmed, embittered, and angry.

Now consider Aunt Betty. She, too, faithfully attended church. Her health is not the best, and she has trouble getting around. Her husband had been sick for a short time. He died in the hospital, and she is sorry that she wasn't able to keep him at home. She is saddened by the fact that her marriage of fifty-five years is over. In her loss, she has fears and concerns, but she recalls their wonderful years together. She considers them a gift and a pleasure. Though saddened, she considers herself blessed. Appreciatively, her family and friends witness her contentment, and Aunt Betty appreciates their concern and help.

Did you notice the radical difference in the responses of these two women? Each was faced with the reality of death and loss. Relationships were changed forever. Their experiences were deeply personal. Both are faced with the reality of being alone, and both have to consider:

- Financial responsibilities, such as paying bills and managing investments
- Household, car, and yard maintenance
- Comforting family members while grieving themselves
- Health issues of their own

In your loss, there will be many people who will want to help and comfort you, and your difficult circumstances may make you more accepting of advice that—though it sounds good on the surface—is not really all that helpful. So what do you do next? What you need is sound, clear, time-proven advice. You need a reliable source of counsel. That source is the Bible. It is the only place to find *joy* in the midst of loss and grief.

This book uses the Bible to address several issues about grief and grieving.

1. Are grief and grieving inevitable?
2. Are grief and grieving necessary? If so, on what basis?
3. Is it possible to grieve in a biblical, God-honoring way?

First, if it is true that grief is inevitable, then it is true that grieving naturally follows. The two are inseparable. Two questions in the Westminster Shorter Catechism address the in-evitability of grief and grieving. Question 17 asks: Into what estate did the Fall bring mankind? Answer: The Fall brought mankind into an estate of sin and misery (Romans 5:12-14). Question 19 asks: What is the misery of that estate whereunto man fell? Answer: By Adam's Fall, all mankind lost commu-nion with God, came under His wrath and curse, and so were made liable to all miseries in this life, to death itself, and to the pains of hell forever (Genesis 3:8-10, 24; Romans 5:12-21, 6:23; Ephesians 2:1-3; Galatians 3:10-13). Death and hell are the ultimate miseries of the lost. The Bible teaches that in our fallen world, sin-cursed bodies make grief and griev-ing inevitable.

Second, the necessity of grief is embrace by our culture. We will see in our survey of a psychological approach to handling life, including the loss of a loved one, that our contemporary culture focuses on the individual who is "left behind." How-ever, we shall see that self-centered grieving does not honor God. Some say that grieving is necessary for "closure." I am not sure what that term means. It is elusive and carries with it an individualistic emphasis. Rather, as discussed above, loss is a consequence of sin due to every person's union with the first Adam and actual sins that flow from that union. How we respond to loss is taught in the Bible. That must be our standard for determining godly grieving in contrast to ungodly grieving.

Third, an essential text is 1 Thessalonians 4:13 (*Brothers, we do not want you to be ignorant about those who fall asleep or grieve like the rest of men who have no hope.*) Clearly, hope anchors the believer's response to loss, and his grieving should contrast with that of the unbeliever. The believer, in grieving God's way, models his Savior and grows in Christlikeness.

Because grief and grieving are inevitable, we need to learn how to grieve God's way and find our joy in grief.

CHAPTER 1

Grief and Grieving

GRIEVING INCLUDES THE FEELINGS AND the responses a person has when faced with serious change or loss. Its context is real-life situations; grief doesn't occur in the abstract or a vacuum. Everyone seems to know what grief is, because all have experienced it in varying forms and degrees.

Change and loss are all around us. People, relationships, circumstances, and lifestyles change. And so do thoughts, desires, hopes, fears, and expectations. For people who don't like change, it is a painful realization that change and loss are common, unavoidable life experiences. In my medical office, patients tell me—often tearfully—about their bodily discomfort and other distresses. The context of their grief may be disease and loss of function, or the loss of a spouse, a family member, a close friend, or even a pet. At church, it is common for people to ask for prayer in regard to their changed situations. My parents used to say that the only two things that didn't change were taxes and death. Since change, loss, and grief are common and almost predictable, it is crucial for us to discover what God says about them.

The Bible teaches that sinless Jesus grieved. Therefore, grieving is appropriate and proper. Furthermore, Scripture clearly teaches that there are two types of grieving: God-honoring and God-dishonoring. Consider 1 Thessalonians 4:13:

> *Brothers, we don't want you to be ignorant about those who fall asleep [die], or to grieve like the rest of men, who have no hope.*

It is clear that some grieved in a despairing way that dishonored God and was of no benefit to the grieving person and his family. Paul expected Christians to grieve hopefully—in a God-honoring way. Therefore, it is important for you to develop a correct perspective on grieving so you may grieve appropriately and properly, thereby glorifying God and benefiting you. This book is meant to help you do that.

In order to accomplish this task, we will look at four main considerations regarding grieving. First, we will contrast the Bible's view with the unbeliever's view of loss, change, and grief.[1] Next, we will focus on Jesus, the model for all of life

---

1   By the term "unbeliever," I am referring to the mindset, perspective on life, set of values and norms, and system of beliefs and behaviors that is competitive with and opposed to biblical truth. In fact, the unbeliever's thinking is part of the "secular world" (a similar term is "the culture"). Mod-

(including grieving). Then, we will consider other examples of grieving—both those that are godly and those that are not. Finally, we will discuss various objections to the Bible's teaching in regard to loss and change. As a result, you will learn how to grieve in a way that is hopeful, purposeful, gracious, compassionate, earnest, and intelligent—that is, appropriate and proper. Grieving God's way is the believer's most gracious and loving act of worship in times of loss.

> *Therefore, I urge you brothers, in view of God's mercy, to offer your bodies as living sacrifices, holy and pleasing to God – this is your spiritual act of worship.*
>
> *Do not conform any longer to the pattern of this world, but be transformed by the renewing of your mind. Then you will be able to test and approve what God's will is –his good, pleasing and perfect will* (Romans 12:1-2).

---

ern society as a whole, and too often the church and the individual believer, has largely abandoned God's way of explaining people, their problems, and providing solutions. Too often, believers and the church function with the same mindset and approach to life as do unbelievers.

CHAPTER 2

The Culture's View of Change, Loss, and Grief

OUR CULTURE HAS MUCH TO say about grief. Webster's Dictionary defines grief as "hardship" and "intense emotional suffering caused by loss, disaster, misfortune, injury, or evils of any kind." Additionally, "to grieve" is to express "emotion at hard times." The word "grief" was originally derived from the Old French word *greve*, meaning "a heavy burden." In English, grief usually indicates an experience of deep sorrow that touches every aspect of one's existence. In short, the grieving person feels weighed down and heavily burdened.

I plugged *grief* into an online search engine and found almost 9.5 million reference sites for grief! Everybody seems to have an idea about the subject and is writing about it. In surveying the websites, it quickly became apparent that psychology and experience are viewed as the best authorities regarding how a person should respond to loss—one of which is "coping."[2] These authorities are the American culture's foundations for developing a philosophy (more accurately a theology) of loss.[3]

If the culture is correct in its assessment, then Christians must follow its message. In fact, many churches, individual believers, organizations (such as Hospice), medical and nursing training programs, and hospital pastoral programs already have done so. If, on the other hand, the culture's premises are incorrect, then believers must move in a radically different direction. Let me summarize what I believe are the culture's leading points regarding change, loss, grief, and grieving.

First, grief is considered from the viewpoint of self. Self takes center stage to the exclusion of others and with no thought of God whatsoever. Frequently, the focus, which continues long after the loss has occurred, appears reasonable

---

2   There are many psychologies. There is no consensus but ever changing proliferation in the psychological world. Psychological theories and therapies differ radically from God's view of man, his problems, and God's solutions as given in Scripture. Far, far too often, those theories and therapies are opposed to and in competition with God and truth.

3   I prefer the term *theology* because life is not neutral. Everyone is a theologian (good or bad) and lives in or out of a proper relationship with God. Therefore, depending on one's relationship with God, he will daily determine truth either based on the Bible or on some counterfeit source of supposed "truth."

since life is radically changed. Grief becomes a driving force in one who considers him or herself a victim, caught in the grip of overwhelming sorrow. Seemingly, something outside takes control. The label of "victim" fits well and sticks. As a result, an agenda for the grieving person is usually developed under the heading of "grief work" or "grief counseling." It is designed to help the grieving one through the "journey of grief and healing" by using a variety of maneuvers such as medications, finding a listener, reconnecting to the lost "other" (person or object), owning the grief, scream therapy, flower energy, and humor.[4] (For a critique of one view, see Appendix D.)

Second, although grief is appreciated as a common experience, the origin of loss and change is viewed incorrectly. Moreover, loss may be viewed as unnatural or even wrong (such as the death of a child). In the Garden of Eden, prior to the Fall of man, grief didn't exist, because sin didn't exist. In the beginning, Adam and Eve did not experience sorrow or loss because everything was very good (Genesis 1:31).

---

4   Here are several websites and the names of some articles that carry this counsel: Discoveryhealth: *How to cope with loss*: www.health.discovery.com; *The grief process*, Judith Kelly: www.thesupportnetwork.net; Rawlings and Kutner, Women's Health in Primary Care: vol. 6, #3, March 2003; *Grieving* by Robert Burney: www.joy2meu.com; *Good Grieving* by Chris Dingle: http://holytrinity.gen.nz; *Coping with loss*: www.helpguide.org; *Grieving God's way*: www.grievinggodsway.com

In a perfect world of no sin, grief doesn't exist. But in our world of sin and sinners, loss is part of our physical life. This is all the more reason that Christians must properly turn to the living God in time of difficulty. Culture gives little consideration to the theological reason for loss and sorrow and the importance of God's grace in grieving God's way. Even if God is considered, He is only viewed as a source of relief from bad feelings.

Psychology is blind to the fact that this is God's world and that He takes care of His people through a relationship with Him in Christ. Psychology does not understand that God provides His Holy Spirit and supplies His sufficient Word for responding to all aspects of life—including change (See 2 Timothy 3:15-17, 2 Peter 1:3-4). Biblical truth, in its entirety, is ignored (and even scorned) because it is considered "inadequate" in handling this "deep issue" of life.

A third emphasis of the culture's non-biblical perspective of grieving is the emotional aspect of the person. Feelings are considered supreme: "you are your feelings." How one feels is treated as if that is the ultimate gauge for judging something to be good or bad. And since "bad feelings" are viewed as detrimental, the goal is to get rid of the bad feelings (see footnote 4). This emphasis on feelings excludes biblically-controlled thinking. Sadly, the church's approach to change, loss, and grief is not much different; pastors, counselors, and even friends focus on the removal of the "bad" feelings rather than on the biblical teaching of pleasing God in all situations.

Fourth, grief and grieving are considered to be a "process," an "experience," and a "journey with several stages" that is "uniquely personal." Grieving is viewed as something that the "victimized" person must go through, and (at the same time) something that he does. Theories abound regarding various models and stages of grief, traveling through the "grief process," adapting, learning to say goodbye, learning to stay connected, and the like.

Lastly, some teach that grief may be lifelong. The bad feelings of grief must be handled by "coping" and "accepting" one's lot in life by whatever way is effective with no hope that it will ever go away. Prolonged grief and grieving may lead to "depression." Therefore, "grief literature" teaches that grief must be dealt with early—even though they believe that grieving may never end. They function by the adage of "once a victim, always a victim." Hope in these circumstances is only a "hope so" hope. This counterfeit hope stands in sharp contrast to biblical hope—a confident expectation of a faithful God keeping His promises for His glory and the believer's good (Roman's 8:28-29).

CHAPTER 3

The Christian's Response

SHOULD THE CHRISTIAN ACCEPT THE culture's understanding and approach to loss? Emphatically, no! Scripture is clear that the believer, and only the believer, can have real hope and confident assurance in God's working all things for His glory and the believer's good (Romans 8:28-29). In evaluating these other approaches to loss and grieving, begin by asking, "Where is there hope in this approach to change and loss?" There is none. In contrast, the Bible has everything to offer grieving people, and here are ten reasons why.

1. **First and foremost, God is the Creator and Designer of man, and He has provided the Bible. And because the Bible is God's manual for life, it is radically superior to any other approach to loss and change. It is all any Christian needs for life and godliness (2 Timothy 3:15-17; 2 Peter 1:3-4).**

**2. Life is theological, and all are theologians. This is so be-
cause God is Creator, and man lives in His world as a dependent, responsible creature. Everyone—believer and
unbeliever alike—lives in or out of a proper relationship
to God. This is true whether acknowledged or not.**

You cannot escape being a theologian; God made you
one. You are either a good theologian or a bad one. How
do you find out which kind you are? By going to Scripture
for the answer (Isaiah 1:10; 5:24; 8:20; 2 Timothy 3:15-
17; 2 Peter 1:3-4). Good theologians acknowledge God's
good and purposeful control of all things. In the case of
change and loss, good theologians must begin with God,
His goodness, and His providential ordering of every single
event in a person's life.

A good theologian is one who understands and lives by
biblical principles as a patterned way of life. He knows and
practices good theology because all problems in life and their
solutions are theological. The circumstances do not determine
his theology. He is not sinless, but he eagerly pursues thinking
God's thoughts, desiring that which pleases God, and acting in
accordance with God's Word. He is a person like David and
Job (1 Samuel 13:14; Job 1:1; 2:3), and even more importantly,
he follows after his Savior Jesus Christ.

Moreover, the good theologian views tough times as the
context in which to correctly apply his theology. To function

as a good theologian in times of loss, one must develop and apply a biblical perspective of change, loss, grief, and grieving. For every believer, understanding who God is and what He is doing brings a different focus to every situation in life.

Luke's words in Acts 2:22–24, 3:13–15, and 4:22–28 help us develop a proper theology of change, loss, and grief. These passages emphasize God's plan of salvation by Christ dying on the cross. Luke focuses on God's control and man's responsibility. Luke leaves no doubt in regard to the ultimate "I don't like" situation (IDLS)—the cross—and God's role in it.[5] God brought about His plan by using man's free choices for the purpose of glorifying Himself and saving a people. Jesus understood His Father's will and was committed to pleasing Him. Jesus was the Ultimate Good Theologian.

---

5   By "I don't like" situations (IDLS), I am referring to the unpleasantness of life – pressure and trouble from the outside that "squeezes" you on the inside. An IDLS is a situation that God brings into a person's life that he would rather not have. There are many situations in life that are hard. Being sinned against is one, and the death of a loved one is another. The key issue in one's response to these situations is a right view of God and His control. Often what makes a situation an IDLS is the person's wrong view of both. is control. There was much unpleasantness in Jesus' life. His goal was to please His Father (John 4:31-34). One lesson of the Cross is to use what one doesn't like to bring about gain in and through the pain. For the believer, the gain is greater Christlikeness.

Focusing on the God of circumstances enables the believer to look away from the unpleasantness of the trouble to God's beneficial purpose in it:

> *And we know that in all things God works for the good of those who love him, who have been called according to his purpose.*
>
> *For those God foreknew he also predestined to be conformed to the likeness of his Son, that he might be the firstborn among many brothers.* (Romans 8:28–29)

The good theologian practices good theology out of gratitude for what God in Christ has done for him personally and God's people corporately. In contrast, a bad theologian lives to please himself, views God as Someone who should supply him with what he wants, and sees himself as deserving God's care and concern (if he considers God at all), especially in times of loss.

3. The nature of man: man is a duplex unit. In regard to man's nature (what he is), the Bible presents man as a unit: he thinks, feels, desires, and doubts both in his inner man (heart) and in his physical body (brain). Originally, God created him a unit consisting of a material, physical body and an inner man. Man has a body, and he is body. But man also has an immaterial side—his inner man. The Bible uses various terms

such as heart, mind, will, conscience, spirit, and soul for the inner man. Man is spirit, but he is more. He is a unit functioning as a whole person.

Man lives out of his heart (Proverbs 4:23; Matthew 12:33-37; Matthew 15:16-20; Mark 7:20-23; Luke 6:43-45). His behavior is an outflow of his inner man where he thinks, evaluates, desires, purposes, hopes, considers, and plans. The Bible doesn't view man's behavior as isolated and unrelated to his inner man. Rather, outer-man and inner-man activities are interrelated. What a person wants—the treasures of his heart—is expressed by actions, desires, and thoughts. This truth is expressed by the phrase "you feel what you feel and you do what you do because you think what you think and want what you want." (Pause and read that again!) Therefore, feelings, actions, thinking, and desires, while separate, are linked together because of man's duplex nature. By changing thinking and desires, a person can change his feelings and actions and thereby his response to any situation, including change and loss.

A person's response to God's providential workings, including loss and change, is a reflection of his wants and motivations—his heart's desires. Consider this illustrative metaphor. When a sponge is squeezed, what is in the sponge comes out. So, too, when man is squeezed by pressures of life (often called stress and stressors), he will demonstrate that which is in him.

Like any response to God's providential workings in his life, when the believer grieves, he expresses the contents of his heart.[6] Since man is a duplex unit functioning out of his heart, his response to any situation will be as a whole person. And because he is a whole person, his thoughts and desires influence the initiation, the intensity, and the duration of grieving.

The specific situation or loss doesn't determine what man's reaction will be. People respond differently to change and loss, as was evident in the lives of Aunt Joan and Aunt Betty. The content, motivation, initiation, expression, and duration of grieving were different for each. The difference was the way in which each one viewed herself in the situation. This assessment is an inner-man activity. Response to loss is dependent on the assessment of several things: a person's view of God, death, and his changed relationship. Unless the believer has a proper biblical perspective of each of those things, he will function as a poor theologian.

You may be wondering how that which is outside of

---

6   By God's providence, I am referring to God actively working out His plan in our lives. God's providence is His personal, preserving, pervasive, and purposeful control of all things that come to pass. In other words, He plans His work and works His plan. God is in control.

you (your circumstances or another person, for example) can cause change on the inside. This question needs to be answered firmly and correctly, because it holds one of the keys for responding to loss in a God-honoring manner. People use different terms for outside pressure and trouble: "hard knocks," "bad luck," "pressure," "stressors," or "stress." These terms all belong in a victim theology. Are people victims at the beck and call of that which surrounds them? The Bible's answer is a resounding *no*. In fact, Paul teaches that Christians are "more than conquerors" *in* (*not* by getting out of) any situation:

> *Who shall separate us from the love of Christ? Shall trouble or hardship or persecution or famine or nakedness or danger or sword? As it is written: for your sake we face death all day long; we are considered as sheep to be slaughtered. No, in all these things we are more than conquerors through Him who loved us* (Romans 8:35-37).

Sound incredulous? How can that be? It is because Jesus Christ is the Ultimate Victor, and every believer is united to Him (Romans 6:9-10; Hebrews 12:1-3). The believer is a new creation, a child of God, and Jesus is his brother (2 Corinthians 5:17; Romans 8:15-17; Hebrews 2:10). He has the Holy Spirit poured into him (Romans 5:5). The believer has a new capacity and power as part of the new creation, which enables him to be victorious even in difficult situations.

4. Everyone functions based on an identity. What he thinks about himself affects his plans, agenda, and pursuits. This is true even when the individual is faced with loss. When a believer identifies himself as a victim or a loser, he is always opposed to God and His truth. Rather, God wants the Christian to think vertically—a correct God focus—and to consider himself as a victor in Christ.

5. Loss is part of life because Adam sinned. The loss of the Garden of Eden and the loss of the righteousness with which Adam was born were fundamental losses for all mankind. Radical change in the form of grief, misery, and sorrow were the outcomes of the first sin (Romans 5:12-14; 2 Corinthians 4:16-18). Therefore, loss of someone (or something) precious is an unavoidable part of living in a fallen world.

6. God's truth and Satan's lies compete. God isn't going bless His competition (Isaiah 42:8; 48:9-11). So believers looking for help outside of God taste only crumbs (the culture's far inferior answer to radical change in life), rather than feasting at the banquet of biblical truth. The culture has developed its own theology of loss and presents a perspective and agenda that is antithetical to God's truth. The cul-

ture is psychologized and medicalized to such an extent that man's wisdom is accepted not only by unbelievers (which is to be expected) but, sadly, by believers as well.[7]

7. God's answers are surpassingly superior, so that when rightly applied, life is simplified, God is glorified, and the grieving believer benefits immensely. He receives the comfort promised in the Scripture and, in time, will comfort others. He is able to function like a Christian oyster, using the hard times to develop the character of Christ. By the terms "Christian oyster" and "using," I am referring to the biblical principle of taking and making an irritant into a lovely thing. The Cross comes to mind. The horror of the cross was transformed by Christ into the greatest good known to mankind. Like the oyster, God gave you, believer, the capacity to transform irritants into pearls. The Christian's pearl is Christlikeness. Becoming more like Christ is the believer's greatest privilege and blessing this side of heaven.

---

7   By the terms "psychologized" and "medicalized," I mean the mindset that assumes non-biblical answers are legitimate alternative explanations and solutions for getting rid of bad "feelings," and that medication is as good as, and perhaps better than, the application of biblical truth. Typically, physicians are quick to prescribe medications in times of loss and grief.

8. **The Bible is about God's control and care of His people. Providentially, God has planned all that comes to pass, hard times and good times, all that happens or doesn't happen in this life (see footnote 6). Humanly speaking, the loss of a loved one is perhaps the ultimate IDLS, but even that loss pales when compared to the Cross. Therefore, it is essential to understand what God has to say about IDLS (this is a crucial point: see footnote 5).**

Any situation may be considered an IDLS, depending on your view of God, self, and the situation. You can either embrace the challenge or reject it as a mistake by God. A proper understanding of God and His sovereign, good, purposeful control promotes hope and encouragement in the midst of hard times, enabling you to function as a good theologian. A Christian who is functioning as a good theologian can grieve in a God-honoring manner uncomplicated by anger, resentment, bitterness, guilt, fear, self-doubt and self-recriminations, and self-pity. These reactions dishonor God and may be triggered or magnified when the focus is on the unpleasantness of the situation.

9. **Change is what the Christian life is all about. The Christian is changed and changing. He is a radically changed person by virtue of God's re-creating ac-**

tivity in his heart called regeneration.[8] Therefore, the Christian is the only one qualified to understand God's purpose in any IDLS and to respond in a God-honoring manner. He can and will function as a good theologian, evaluating all of life from God's perspective as taught in His Word. As a result, he will focus on God's presence, purpose, and promises rather than the unpleasantness of the situation.

Not only is the believer a most changed person, he is a uniquely changing person. All believers are "becomers." This process is called sanctification.[9] As new creatures in Christ, they are in the process of changing more and more into the likeness of Christ (2 Corinthians 5:9; Romans 8:28-29; 2 Corinthians 3:18). Becoming more like Christ is God's design for believers, is best for them, and is the only way for them to live satisfying lives (Ephesians 1:4). Unfortunately,

---

8   Regeneration is the change produced by the Holy Spirit in the heart of man. The person's heart of stone is made a heart of flesh, responsive to the things of God (Ezekiel 36:26; John 3:3-6; 1 Corinthians 2:10-16). Regeneration now enables him to repent and believe in the person and work of Jesus Christ.

9   Sanctification is the process in which every believer dies more and more to self and lives more and more to God. It is the work of God's free grace whereby the Christian, in his whole person, begins more and more to think God's thoughts, to desire what God desires, and to act as a God-pleaser rather than as a self-pleaser.

most believers find it difficult in hard times, especially in loss, to acknowledge and act upon that truth.

Times of loss are an opportunity for you to turn from self-dependence and to a greater reliance on God (Romans 5:1-5; James 1:2-4; 1 Peter 1:6-7; 2 Corinthians 1:8-10). God has created and re-created His people with the ability and capacity to depend on Him and thereby be blessed. That means in good times and hard times, God expects you and enables you to develop contentment, practice trust, and faithfully depend on Him and His faithfulness (1 Corinthians 10:13; Philippians 4:10-13).

Trouble and loss don't change a person or cause him to think, desire, or act in a certain way. As I have said, the believer is not a victim but *more* than a conqueror (Romans 8:35-37). The key is his response to trouble. His response reflects his inner man. His response is a whole-person activity that includes his thinking, desires, and feelings, and his actions toward God, self, others, and the trouble.

It is easy in the midst of trouble to focus on self and the problem. In order for the believer to respond in a godly manner, it is essential for him to meditate on the truth that God is infinitely trustworthy and His control is good (Philippians 4:8,13). The believer is called to trust God in every circumstance, including personal loss, and to prove trustworthy by functioning as a Christian oyster.

10. Jesus and the Cross provide important biblical principles to guide us in developing a theology of and a proper response to change and loss. Given its significance, the next section expands the Bible's teaching of Jesus as our example and how He grieved.

CHAPTER 4

Jesus, the Believer's Model

NOW WE ARE READY TO examine the Bible's specific teaching regarding loss, change, grief, and grieving. It is encouraging and instructive to realize that God has given full attention to this matter. *Lupeo* (verb) and *lupe* (noun) are the most common Greek words translated as grief and grieve in the New Testament. [10] Both carry the meaning and expression of sadness, sorrow, pain, and anguish. Biblically speaking, grief is the God-given capacity to sorrow as a result of a significant loss. Grief and its expression flow from thinking and wanting. As a result of loss, a person chooses to think a certain way, which—depending upon the direction of those thoughts—produces thoughts, feelings, and behaviors that honor or dishonor God.

---

10   Scripture attests to God's concern for grieving people, in part, by using a variety of words that are translated as "grief, grieve, mourning, or sadness." See Appendices A and B.

The earliest explanation of pain in Scripture is given in Genesis 3. Pain and grief are the result of Adam's sin and man's Fall with him (Genesis 3:15-18). Yet God in these verses makes it clear that pain and sorrow should not stand alone. From the beginning, the bad news of man's fallen condition and the resultant misery was inexorably linked to the reality of the good news—the gospel message of salvation through the coming Messiah. In the midst of pain and sorrow, God promised joy and, in Christ, He delivered (Genesis 3:15-18; Proverbs 14:13; Isaiah 35:1-10; 51:1-16; 61:1-3; Habakkuk 3:16-19; John 16:20-22). Truly, this link is hope engendering.

You may be thinking, "How can something that hurts so badly be linked to good news? How can something that hurts so much be beneficial?" Great questions! Though the Roman cross represented horror, humiliation, and death, to the Christian it is the power and wisdom of God (Romans 1:16; 1 Corinthian 1:18, 21, 24). At the cross, Christ demonstrated God's goodness, mercy, and justice by saving His people. Man's salvation glorifies God because God did what was impossible for man to do—save unlovable and wretched sinners who would become lovers of God and others.

As we consider Christ and the Cross, keep in mind that loss is part of life in a fallen world. Loss rightly responded to, brings great benefit. However, wrong responses produce only

aggravation and discontentment, and of greater significance—
they dishonor God.

In Scripture, there are several examples of Jesus' grieving,
and certain characteristics of His grief and grieving are worthy
of note. These include the initiation and content of grief; the
motive, manner, and magnitude of grieving; the duration of
grieving; and whether grieving is "complicated" or not.

These passages give insight into Jesus' thoughts and feelings as the sinless, sacrificial, sin-bearing Substitute. In them,
we find that the words used for grief and grieving in Jesus'
case are not the usual ones. I believe that the usual words
(*lupe/lupeo*) simply don't do justice to the content, motivation, and magnitude of Jesus' grief. From these passages, we
will glean God's hopeful and victorious truths that will help
you grieve His way.

John 11: Grieving over Lazarus

Consider chapter 11 of John's Gospel. John records the
death of Lazarus and the responses of various people, including Jesus. In verse 4, Mary and Martha sent word to Jesus that
their brother Lazarus was ill. However, Jesus lingered for two
days longer and then in Bethany found Lazarus dead in the
tomb for four days (verse 6, 17). Verse 19 says, "and many Jews
had come to Mary and Martha to console them about their
brother." Jewish practices of mourning in the Old and New
Testament, while similar, differed from our modern practices

in America. It was customary to mourn visibly and loudly, and professional mourners were often used for that purpose (Matthew 9:23). But here in John 11, Jesus preferred to weep quietly (verse 35, "Jesus wept").

Verse 33 says, "When Jesus saw her weeping, and the Jews who had come along with her also weeping, he was deeply moved in spirit and troubled," and verse 38 tells us that Jesus again was "stirred within, troubled, and deeply moved." The two words used to describe His response are *embrimaomai* and *tarasso*. The first word indicates righteous indignation, and both words express an agitation of the inner person.[11] There was much "noise" in Jesus' heart—He was troubled and agitated within. Sandwiched between these two verses is verse 35: "Jesus wept." Here, the word is *dakruo,* which means the physical act of shedding a tear and is used only here in the New Testament. It stands in contrast to the common word for crying and the expression of grief especially in response to death—*klaio* (this word is the word translated as "weeping" in verse 33).

What more are we to learn from these passages in John 11?

---

11   *Embrimaomai* has the idea of roaring within in response to something outside of one's self. It indicates an inner person activity: Matthew 9:30; Mark 1:43; 14:5; John 11:33, 38. *Tarasso* indicates a stirring up within, inward agitation, and being troubled within: John 11:33; 12:27; 13:21;14:1, 27; Matthew 2:3;14:26; Mark 6:50; Luke 1:12; 24:38; 1 Peter 3:14.

1. **Appropriate and proper grieving is to be pure and unadulterated without fear, bitterness, and resentment; it is to be informed by God's ultimate purpose in life and death—salvation through the Cross for His glory. In this way, it will be rightly motivated and *uncomplicated*. As we have mentioned, God-honoring grief is vertically focused. Grief that is purposeful will move the believer toward God, not away from Him, and will enable him to minister and to be ministered to in times of loss. God-honoring grief will not be complicated by anger, bitterness, and resentment; these reactions are ultimately directed at God because of His control of all of life.**

Lazarus had died, and Jesus and others were sorrowful. Jesus' weeping was considered by the Jews to be a sign that Jesus truly cared about Lazarus. (Verse 36, "So the Jews said, 'Look at how He cared for him!'") Godly grieving is genuinely compassionate and is visible. It is not a stoic, cold statement that God will do whatever He wants, whenever He wants, and all we need to do is "grin and bear it" or "just deal with it."

2. **The death of Lazarus offered a preview of the Cross. Jesus had lost a friend, and He grieved as a whole person, being moved within. But what was Jesus' grief all about? He was grieving at the fact of sin and its consequences—misery and death. He was angered over**

the effects of sin because He fully understood God's wrath, the cost of removing it, and His role in doing so. He was troubled because He was to incur the full measure of God's unmitigated wrath in order to reverse the curse of sin.

Moreover, His desire to please His Father would enable Him to endure death on the cross (John 4:31-34; Hebrews 12:1-3). Jesus understood loss as no one else could. Yet, He chose to please His Father by facing death as the Redeemer and Justifier in order to remove the consequences of Adam's sin (Romans 3:21-26; 4:25). Jesus, the perfect man, had the proper understanding of life, which led to a correct motivation for perfect grieving. At the cross, He was about to experience the greatest loss, a loss that you and I never will undergo. His humiliation would soon be complete. He was to be forsaken by His Father. Jesus viewed the loss of His friend in terms of His greater loss. He grieved—but not without hope. What was His anchor?

Jesus knew full well of God's initial promise in the Garden of Eden: in the midst of misery and sin, there was joy (Genesis 3:15-18). His grief was always linked to joyful gain. At this point in His ministry, He gave a preview of one of the effects of the Cross: resurrection. Jesus was not simply a crucified Savior—He is the Resurrected Savior! The ultimate comfort in this life and the next is both Jesus' and the believer's resurrection (1 Corinthians 15:19-20; 1 Thessalonians 4:14). Jesus' grieving was balanced by the joy of His exaltation that would begin with His resurrection.

3. **The content, initiation, expression, and duration of grief and grieving must be in accordance with biblical truth. Jesus knew His origin, destiny, and His task on earth. He knew that His return to the Father would only come after the Cross. In His humiliation, He looked forward to the gain. His relationship with the Father and the expectation of His victorious return to heaven motivated Him to grieve with an eternal perspective. He taught this same truth to Martha (John 11:23-27). As believers, knowing our origin (chosen in Him in eternity past), our destiny (growth in Christ on earth and being in God's presence forever), and our purpose in life (pleasing God) influences the "how," the "duration," and the "motivation" of our grieving (Ephesians 1:4; Romans 8:28-29; 1 John 3:1-3).**

The principle is this: the assessment of the loss and its impact on the person left behind is a major factor in how people grieve. Any assessment involves the person's perception of the importance of the one lost, the relationship severed, and his life after the loss. The greater the value placed on the person (or the object) that is gone and the greater the cost to the person left behind, the greater the potential effect of the loss.

Some practical implications in time of loss include, but are not limited to, the following:

- Consider taking some extra time to decide "what now." Wise decision-making pleases God, so please don't keep your over-committed pace. Take the time to give some thought to where you will go and what you will do.

- Consider taking a break from such things as teaching Sunday school or choir practice—these are reasonable choices as you have other immediate responsibilities.

- Even so, it is not okay to fail to use your gifts for the body of Christ. Having taken a reasonable amount of time to make wise, biblical decisions and find comfort in Christ, please remember that God has work for you—to continue to function as a helpful and hopeful member of the body of Christ.

- And it is not OK to neglect God-given responsibilities. You may still have a job, children, or family members to care for, or other responsibilities that cannot and must not be neglected, even though you are grieving.

As a corollary, you and I must face our losses with the hope (confident expectation) that Jesus had. His was an informed hope. He knew that Lazarus' death was ultimately for the glory of God (John 11:4). Therefore, He knew how to interpret loss. For the believer, loss in this life is temporary, is always to be compared to the benefit and gain, and is ultimately for the eternal good of a believer. Loss, rightly responded to, points to that which is supremely valuable: God's relationship with him. Viewing loss through one's relationship with Christ enables the believer to grieve God's way.

Moreover, when rightly viewed by the believer, loss points to heaven. What Jesus lost on earth, He gained manifold in heaven—glorification (Hebrews 12:1-3). The way to heaven for Jesus was the cross. There was no other way. As He faced death, Jesus looked beyond the cross and pain to His Father in heaven, which was true gain and true glory. Raising Lazarus from the dead was a preview of that gain and glory. In the middle of pain and sorrow, Jesus brought joy. Because of His eager anticipation, Jesus did not allow His grieving to become complicated. He was not deterred from His mission, nor was He swallowed up in grief. In fact, grief motivated Him to go to the cross in order to complete His mission. He knew that the cross was God's instrument for the reversal of that which produces grief. In situations of loss, the believer needs to have Jesus' perspective not only of the cross but the glory beyond the cross.

In the same way, the reality of the resurrection should enable the believer to know God's goodness in hard times. *But we do not want you to be ignorant about those who fall asleep or to grieve like the rest of men who have no hope* (1 Thessalonians

4:13). One way to do so is to enjoy the ministry of God's grace brought through other believers. The one who grieves should focus on what God is providing for him in the situation rather than on his loss.

Caring concern begins in the body of Christ. It is the way that the world knows who Jesus' disciples are (John 13:34-35; Galatians 6:10). Just as the physical body has many parts, so too the Church, the body of Christ, has many members. All parts and members are needed for health and proper function (Romans 12:3-8; 1 Corinthians 12:12-27). Within the body, a good God has provided people with various gifts, including the gifts of service, hospitality, and mercy. Thankfully acknowledge and receive God's goodness as others comfort you. In this way, you and others will be encouraged and strengthened, and God will be glorified. In time, you will be restored and look forward to comforting others with God's comfort as you have been comforted (2 Corinthians 1:3-4).

When Aunt Sarah, a professing Christian, lost four family members in one year, one of whom was her mother, she thought that God had taken her best friends, people she depended on. Her mother was "high maintenance," but Aunt Sarah had diligently cared for her for years. Aunt Sarah told the family that she felt overwhelmed. In her losses, she wondered and fretted about what she would do now, and she thought that no one understood her feelings and situation. She reported that her husband told her to "get a grip," and the grief counselor told her that death is "natural—everybody dies. Death just is."

Aunt Sarah told me about her life of "so many demands on me" and "little resources." She said, "I know it is selfish, but I can't help thinking about Mother all the time. I can't quit focusing on the loss. The grief counselor told me it was OK to feel this way. I am clinging to things that I don't have—what am I going to do?"

What was going on with Aunt Sarah? For Sarah, happiness was defined as "right now," and it came from "self-fulfillment"—the "I wantsies." Now she was out of her comfort zone, and she didn't like it. She was correct: she was being selfish. She blamed God for her losses. Wallowing in self-pity, she felt hopeless and helpless. The crucified, resurrected, victorious Savior and her apparent relationship with Him had no impact on her response to her circumstances. In effect, all that had been gained in Christ was "undone" by her losses, desire for relief, and bad feelings.

The believer's loss and grieving is always to be balanced with the joy of resurrection life that begins on this earth. Both Aunt Sarah and Aunt Joan had a shortsighted view of life. Both focused on the losses and what they were missing in this life. Consequently, they produced more pain and misery for themselves and others. Loss of any magnitude is to be used as God's instrument for becoming more like Christ, which is possible only because of Jesus' loss (the cross) and His gain (resurrection). 1 John 3:3 gives an eternal perspective for life. John wrote that the promised hope of seeing God face to face should be a prime, daily, motivating factor for becoming more like Christ. The joy of eternal life can begin even now for the believer.

While grieving over Lazarus, Jesus looked away from self and toward others because His focus was on the eternal gain. He ministered to grieving Martha and Mary by pointing them to Himself and the great truth that He is the great "I Am," the Resurrection and the Life (11:23-32). Jesus raised Lazarus from the dead as a preview of His work on the Cross—death was swallowed up, and its stinger removed—which is the beginning of resurrection life here on earth (Romans 6:9-10; 1 Corinthians 15:54-57). The hope of resurrection life enables the believer to grieve God's way, not fearing death or loss.

Matthew 26:38 and Mark 13:34: Grieving in the Garden

Consider the parallel passages **Matthew 26:38** (*Then He said to them, "My soul is deeply grieved, even to the point of death. Stay here and watch with Me,"*) and **Mark 14:34** (*Then He said to them, "I am so upset I am at the point of death. Stay* *here and watch with Me"*).[12] These verses depict Jesus in His anguish the night before He died. Jesus had faced many IDLS throughout His life as part of His humiliation.[13] Now He faced the ultimate IDLS—separation from His Father as the Mediator (Christ stands between the Father and His people as Savior and Sin-bearer) of His people. His humiliation was about to be complete both physically—a humiliating, almost incomprehensible, horrible death, and spiritually—going to hell on the cross by being separated from the Father.

He had left heaven and all its splendor and majesty to

---

12   *Perilupos,* used in these two passages referring to Jesus' anguish, is used only two others times: Mark 6:26 in reference to Herod Antipas when he was faced with murdering John the Baptist in order to remain true to his promise, and in Luke 18:23 when the rich young ruler was deeply grieved when faced with the choice of full-hearted allegiance to Christ. Their heightened grief was on the basis of their self-centered approach to life. They focused on self and their personal loss.

13   Humiliation is defined by question 27 of the Westminster Shorter Catechism and is based on the following passages: Luke 2:7; Galatians 4:4; Isaiah 53:3; Matthew 27:46; Philippians 2:6-8; 1 Corinthians 15:4. Jesus' humiliation consisted in His leaving heaven and His rightful place of honor and glory to be born in a low condition and made under the law. He underwent the miseries of life on earth as the God-man, the wrath of God, and the cursed death of the cross. He was then buried and remained under the power of death until His resurrection.

live as a "misfit" and a "no-account"—just another Jew
(Isaiah 52:14-53:4). Jesus had a major, radical change in
His existence that is unparalleled in human history. In His
humiliation, Jesus' grieving differs from yours and mine
not only in degree and magnitude but in its very nature.
Separation from His Father loomed large before Jesus as He
set His face toward Jerusalem (Luke 9:51). Jesus' grieved as
He focused on His separation—something believers will
never experience. That fact alone should help to motivate
every believer to grieve with hope.

As Jesus anticipated bearing the full weight of God's wrath,
He described Himself as being "deeply grieved" and, in another translation, being "overwhelmed with sorrow." The
word that is translated in these phrases is *perilupos*, which is
a heightened form of grief (*lupe*). Yet, in the midst of deep
hurts and anguish, Jesus is vertically focused. He is alone in
prayer with the Father, communicating His ultimate desire
to please Him.

Moreover, the cross with its pain and misery didn't catch
Jesus by surprise. When faced with loss, and cherishing His
relationship with the Father, He knew He was not alone
(John 8:16, 8:29; 16:32). The truth of His vital relationship with the Father impacted how He viewed life and the
way He grieved. Because of His intimate relationship with
the Father, He was able to grieve without self-pity, bitter-

ness, resentment, fear, or disobedience. He was prepared to face His ultimate IDLS with informed, joyful grieving. Again, Scripture highlights Jesus' sinless example of grieving, which teaches that grieving is appropriate and proper, and it is to be informed, purposeful, and uncomplicated. Therefore, there is a place for grieving in the believer's life, and it can and should be God honoring (see 1 Thessalonians 4:13).

Jesus did not waver as He moved toward the cross, completely relying on His Father even when His disciples deserted Him after vowing never to do so (Matthew 26:31–35, 56; Mark 14:32–42; Luke 22:40–46). Moreover, fully trusting His Father, Jesus remained on the cross for those hours when darkness filled the land (Matthew 27:45–46). Scripture is silent about this time. What transpired between the Son and the Father is unknown. Apparently, it was complete separation from His Father as He went to hell on the cross. Even the Father had to turn His back on the God-man Jesus in payment for the sins of His people. And yet, Jesus, truly God, was still able to cry out to His Father, "My God, my God, why have you forsaken Me?" (Matthew 27:46). The question reflects the magnitude of the depth of Jesus' anguish! Jesus knew the answer. Separation from the Father secured His Father's pleasure and gained a people for Himself. Jesus' grief moved Him to victory.[14] Life, let alone grieving, was not a process or journey for Jesus. His grieving was purposeful, and so it can be for us as we learn to view hardships as God's tool for completing His work in our lives—bringing about Christlikeness.

Jesus was no mere martyr or victim. He was the Lord of lords and King of kings, the Lamb of God who, out of His desire to please His Father, bore the wrath of God on behalf of His people (John 1:29, 36; 2 Corinthians 5:21). Rather than focusing on the pain and anguish, Jesus focused on the joy set before Him:

> *Therefore, since we are surrounded by such a great cloud of witnesses, let us throw off everything that hinders and the sin that so easily entangles, and let us run with perseverance the race marked out for us. Let us fix our eyes on Jesus, the author and perfecter of our faith, who for the joy set before him endured the cross, scorning its shame, and sat down at the right hand of the throne of God. Consider him who endured such opposition from sinful men so that you will not grow weary and lose heart.*
> (Hebrews 12:1-3)

In the midst of pain and misery, Jesus displayed an unbe-

---

14   No mention is made of the Father's reaction in Scripture. Did He grieve? One can only wonder regarding the dynamic between the Father and Son in those dark hours.

lievable, even mind-boggling, focus on pleasing His Father and ministering to His sheep. He had a proper vertical and horizontal reference to life. [15] In the Garden, by focusing on His mission, He was able to encourage and warn His three companions to pray and not to fall into temptation (Matthew 26:36-46; Mark 14:32-42; Luke 22:40-46). On the cross, He ministered to His mother, John, the thief on the cross, and He even prayed to the Father for the salvation of His enemies. He remained there for us. His circumstances did not alter His motivation or concern for others. Rather, they stimulated in Him an intense desire to finish the race, please His Father, and obtain the crown set before Him.

By way of contrast, consider the rich young ruler. He, like Christ, had a choice: hold on to riches or give allegiance to God (Luke 18:23). His inner turmoil was an expression of his "me-approach" to life. He mourned selfishly. He mourned not because he was to suffer separation from God (though he would be eternally separated from Him unless he repented), but because he would be separated from "stuff"—his true god—that he thought and hoped would make him happy.

---

15   The concept of vertical and horizontal reference to life is taken from Matthew 22:37-40. In answering the question of which is the greatest commandment, Jesus answered by focusing His listeners vertically (the love of the Father) and horizontally (love of neighbor). Jesus knew that sinners, both saved and unsaved, are self-focused and lovers of self.

Ironically, his desire and pursuit of that desire would only bring hardship (Proverbs 13:15).

Notice the contrast between Jesus' grief and that of the rich young ruler. Both grieved at the prospect of loss and change. Yet the content, focus, and object of Jesus' grief was entirely different from the ruler's. The young man's attention was a self-focus centering on what his loss would cost him—he saw no gain in his loss. Jesus also counted the loss, but He viewed it as gain. His Father would receive His people, and Jesus would receive His rightful place with the Father as exalted King of kings and Lord of lords. His eternal perspective and vertical focus motivated Him to bear the temporal loss for the eternal gain.

In the final analysis, Jesus focused on His relationship with the Father, thereby continuing His course toward the cross. The ruler focused on himself and ultimately, by ignoring Christ's message, missed out on a glorious eternity. Jesus teaches us that grieving God's way is always cross-centered, viewing His circumstances in light of the cross. He remained faithful to pleasing His Father by fulfilling His responsibilities and ministering to others out of love and gratitude for His relationship with the Father.

As a result of Christ's work at the cross, the believer will never face God's wrath as the Just Judge. Jesus did that for you—in your place, as your Substitute! Personal loss allows the believer to better understand and appreciate the loss that Jesus chose to suffer on his behalf. An understanding of this kind of love will allow the believer to grieve in a God-honoring manner.

Moreover, in America, the believer's struggle with sin and loss will probably not require him to shed blood—at least not in the near future (Hebrews 12:4). Yet, when faced with loss, the believer should compare his situation with Jesus' humiliation. Jesus faced trouble throughout His entire life and showed His people how to grieve. Jesus, our great High Priest, so identified with His people that He is called a man who was "acquainted with grief" (Hebrews 4:15; Isaiah 53:3). Because of Jesus' model and the believer's relationship with Him, the believer can and must grieve as a good theologian.

As a closing caveat to this section, we often think that others cannot know the full extent of our hurts, our thoughts, and our feelings. There is a desire, even a demand, for someone to understand. Yet, God knows and understands. Therefore, rightly focused, the Christian will joyfully and correctly understand who Jesus is, the cost Jesus paid, and the revolting horror of sin. In response, the believer should be driven to the Cross and a right view of his relationship to God, who understood His Son's grief. If He understands His Son and His humiliation, He certainly understands you, believer.

Luke 19:41-42; 23:28: Grieving over the City

Our last set of passages is found in Luke's Gospel. *Now as He drew near, He saw the city and wept over it saying, "if even today you knew what would bring peace! But now it is hidden from your eyes"* (Luke 19:41-42). As Jesus approached Jerusalem, He looked at the city and wept and loudly grieved (*klaio*). His tears of grief were not for Himself, as many scholars would have us believe. Rather, Jesus wept because He completely understood the true sense of man's lost condition—man's deadness, the darkness of the kingdom of Satan, the insurmountable distance between God and man, man's infinite indebtedness to God without any hope or means of payment, and the consequences for those continuing in unrepentant sin.

Later in his account, Luke recorded that Jesus wanted others to grieve over the city. Several women were gathered along the way as Jesus went to His crucifixion, and they were weeping for Jesus. Jesus told them that their object of weeping (*klaio*) was wrong. *Then Jesus turned and said to them, "Daughters of Jerusalem, don't weep for Me. Weep for yourselves and your children"* (Luke 23:28). Jesus exhorts, even rebukes, these women because their grieving was misdirected. It should not have been for Him but for themselves. And, moreover, their grieving should have been balanced by the joy of His victory on the cross.

What did Jesus mean by "weeping for oneself"? The phrase

sounds like secular counsel—"grief work."The women were moved by the sight of Jesus and His "plight." But they pictured Him and the cross strictly from a human perspective. Their hopes had been shattered, the Messiah had not come, and though Jesus was a nice man, He was a "loser." They failed to view what was happening from God's perspective. They did not understand that it was their own sinfulness that demanded a full payment on the cross.They failed to see the need of repentance.

The majority of Jerusalem's population consisted of those who had rejected the Messiah and His plan of salvation.They were in desperate need of repentance (Matthew 23:37-38; Luke 13:34-35). Terrible woes were to befall the city of Jerusalem if Israel failed to repent. So the only hope the women, and all of Israel, had for obtaining joy was through repentance.[16]

As we ponder Christ at the cross, we learn that responses to hard situations, including loss, have both a vertical and horizontal reference. Christ, the Ultimate Theologian, is the believer's model for properly responding to IDLS. A right view of Christ and the Cross motivates the Christian to think vertically as he focuses on God and His glory, and to think horizontally as he considers the loss, his response, and those around him.When the believer uses the loss to become more

---

16   James 4:7-10; Proverbs 28:13; Psalm 32 and 38

like Christ, he is responding as a good theologian—and a Christian oyster.

Additionally, our crucified Savior teaches us a basic biblical truth: that which glorifies

God is for the benefit of the believer (Genesis 50:19-21; Romans 8:28-29). The two—God's glory and the believer's benefit—are inextricably tied together. Joy will always be available in the midst of grief if the believer will develop and maintain an eternal gaze as Christ did—looking to the final outcome. Grieving God's way is cross-centered, always requiring an eye on the Cross and looking toward heaven.

So how does Jesus' counsel to "weep for oneself" apply to us? First, a person should acknowledge the curse of sin as the cause of all misery, death, and loss on this earth (Romans 5:12-14). Then he should confess any known sin (James 5:14-16). In essence, "weeping for oneself" means counting the cost by recognizing and acknowledging that Jesus had to humiliate Himself as the Savior of His people and die in the place of undeserving rebels.

Though death itself has not been removed, the power and sting of death have been (1 Corinthians 15:54-57; Hebrews 2:14-17). Therefore, believer, even in loss, tears of joy can flow when you firmly hold on to the truth that you are counted as one of His! In your loss, you are not alone (Hebrews 13:5-

6).Your trustworthy God forsook His Son so that you would never be alone!

In summary, think back to the introduction and the two women. Which one modeled Christ in her loss? Which one focused on the Cross? Each lady was a theologian, but only one was a good one (Aunt Betty). Aunt Joan complicated her loss and sorrow with anger, bitterness, resentment, and discontent. Her response dishonored God and brought misery to herself and others. She was a poor theologian. Aunt Betty simply grieved—she hurt. She expressed thankfulness for the years together with her husband, and she was grateful for the care and help of family and friends in the midst of her sorrow. She was a good theologian by responding to hard times in a God-honoring manner.

CHAPTER 5

Application of the Principle of Gain through Loss

THE GUIDING PRINCIPLE OF GAIN through loss should characterize the life of every believer just as it did for Jesus and Paul. As we have emphasized, Christ's humiliation describes His immeasurable loss. Christ voluntarily and temporarily set aside the rights and privileges of all that to which He was entitled as God and gave full attention to what He would gain (Philippians 2:5-8). Theologians speak of Christ's gain as His exaltation, which consisted of His resurrection, ascension, placement in heaven at the right hand of the Father, and His imminent return as the Just Judge of the earth.[17] Jesus understood that the pain, rightly responded to, was producing gain. As such, He was able to give full

---

17   Taken from question 28 of the Westminster Shorter Catechism and the following passages: 1 Corinthians 15:4; Acts 1:9; Ephesians 1:20; Acts 1:11; 17:31.

attention to His earthly task, knowing that His gain would be exceedingly and surpassingly great.

What sustained Him in His humiliation? As we said previously, it was His relationship to His Father and the Father's to Him. Therefore, Jesus' attention was on what His loss was producing for Himself, His Father, and His people. Relationships do matter, especially in tough times! In his Gospel, John makes clear that Jesus was discipled by the Father, which enabled Him to remain faithful to His mission. He did nothing on His own and acknowledged His dependence on the Father by reflecting the Father's teaching.[18] As the Father's Disciple and Son, Jesus learned obedience through suffering, which prepared Him to be Mediator and High Priest for the benefit of His people (Hebrews 2:10; 5:8; 4:15).[19] Loss had been

---

18   John 4:34; 5:19-20,30; 6:38; 8:26, 28-29; 9:4; 10:37-38; 12:49-50; 14:31; 15:10; 17:4. His disciples were to imitate Him.

19   Jesus was the Mediator between God and His people, and this was unique to Him. His perfect life and perfect death earned God's favor for His people. His life and death enabled God to justify the unjust, declaring the guilty innocent by reckoning Christ's righteous life and death to His people (Romans 3:21-26; 4:5-8; 8:1, 32-34). God was glorified in the only way possible. The Cross clearly demonstrated that God is both good and loving, while also powerful and just (Psalm 62:11-12). As Mediator, Jesus experienced the human condition – its sufferings, loss, and sorrow – in its fullest, yet He was without sin (Hebrews 4:15). Therefore, He mediated on behalf of suffering believers. He was God's man and your Savior, Redeemer, and Friend.

an integral part of Jesus' earthly life, and His ultimate loss, to be forsaken by His Father, was imminent. Yet His loss, rightly responded to, would produce the perfect gain: resurrection for Himself and His people (Romans 6:9-10; 8:28-29; 1 Corinthians 15:54-57). Jesus grieved and practiced the ultimate trust because His grief directed Him toward God.

As we have noted and as hard as it may be at the time, a proper perspective of loss means that Christ's loss was far greater than the believer's. That is not to say that the believer's loss is insignificant—quite the contrary. But as hard as any loss may be, it pales in contrast to Jesus' loss. That statement is a theological truth of gigantic proportions not easily accepted or acted upon (remember aunts Joan and Sarah).

In His humiliation, Jesus' grieving differs from yours and mine not only in degree and magnitude but in its very nature. Separation from His Father loomed large before Jesus as He set His face toward Jerusalem (Luke 9:51). Jesus' grief focused on that separation—something believers will never experience. Correctly viewed, His loss is your loss, and His gain is your gain. And more, your loss is for the purpose of producing gain that is true victory.

Paul, an imitator of Christ, also knew the power of gain through loss (1 Corinthians 11:1). He recorded his personal evaluation of Christ's teaching in Philippians 3:3-11. When Paul became a Christian, he acknowledged that he had lost much: pedigree, position, preeminence, power, peace, and prosperity. But his loss was more than physical and cultural standing—foremost, it was self-reliance. As a result, Paul was able to consider his relationship with Christ as real gain that was surpassingly superior to what he had formerly held dear; what he had considered gain, he now considered as loss. Paul had learned one of the lessons of the Cross, and he continued to apply it daily. No wonder Paul urged the Thessalonians to grieve in a God-honoring way.

The "gain" is achieved when loss and change are viewed as the means that God uses to bring about new growth through an increasing reliance on Him, a greater appreciation of one's relationship to God in Christ, and an increasing, eternal perspective (2 Corinthians 4:16-18; 5:7; 1 John 3:1-3).[20] In God's providence, when a Christian is stripped of what he considers valuable and important, he is faced with a decision: he can place his confidence and trust in himself, others, and situations, or in Christ and His Word. What did Jesus do? He clung to His Father, depending on that relationship to sustain Him. As a result, He was motivated to fight the good fight, to run the race with endurance, and to persevere to the end. And He did!

---

20   In these verses, Paul speaks of inner-man renewal. The believer's changed heart began at salvation, and the "changing" continues daily as he grows in Christlikeness. Failing and dying bodies are the context for him to do that.

Similarly, when you acknowledge and act on your relationship to God in Christ, you will experience great gain—growing in Christlikeness. And this growth leads to the greatest gain—being in the presence of God forever.

Practically speaking, living out one's relationship to Christ means several things:

1. It means that you are growing and changing by using hard times to do so. When hard times occur, therefore, they are not to be avoided, feared, denied, or allowed to become a source of bitterness and resentment. Rather, IDLS are to be seen as part of God's plan for good.

2. It means that you are to be content in the situation, and not inordinately desiring to have relief from it by having it removed (Romans 8:35–37). Victory comes even in the midst of hard times.

3. It means using the IDLS to please God even when you don't feel like it. One way this may occur is by choosing to trust God rather than your feelings, even though things are bad.[21]

4. It means accepting help in hard times. That is not always easy to do, especially if you are someone who

---

21   I define trust as reading, understanding, believing, submitting to, and correctly applying God's Word/truth that is appropriate for you and your situation.

is used to being relatively self-sufficient.

    5. It means looking for ways to serve others when you think and feel that you can't.

People often count the cost in terms of their loss rather than their gains. It is easy for a person to measure his loss and judge his situation based on what he doesn't have. However, in order to grieve God's way, every believer must *rethink* life without _____ (fill in the blank).

At some point in life, everyone will lose someone or something that is considered valuable. In response, some people may say that they can't live without whatever it was they held dear. The Bible never denies the reality of the miseries accompanying life in a fallen world, but biblical truth is not an anesthetic to numb your hurts. The Cross speaks to this loud and clear. Jesus stood strong and firm by pleasing the Father, going to the cross, and restraining Himself when opposed by sinners and His family. So too, believers are able to please the Father when it seems impossible, illogical, or impractical (Hebrews 12:1-3; Mark 3:20-35). This is victory *in* the IDLS, not out of it.

Returning to Romans 8:35-39, you are more than a conqueror in Christ. These words mean that you can respond to your loss by looking past the pain to the gain. Christ did it in your place, as your Substitute, in a magnificently glorious way. He bids you to come follow Him. Armed with the Holy

Spirit, God's promises, and His grace, you too will endure as a victor. You can do all things through Christ who strengthens you (Philippians 4:13). Therefore, be encouraged, believer!

CHAPTER 6

The Death of an Unbeliever

THE DEATH OF AN UNBELIEVING loved one is a reality. Can there be joy in these losses for the believer? Can there be God-honoring grieving? The biblical principles that we have learned hold true even for these losses. No matter the loss, grief and grieving will be appropriate, proper, and uncomplicated when the believer remembers and acts on the truth that God has answers, and that those answers are best for him in any situation.

The loss of a loved one is an IDLS in which a believer may be tempted to question, protest, or deny the providential goodness of God. As was stated earlier, the good theologian remains a victorious Christian by remembering that this is God's world, that God is good, that He loves each individual believer intimately, that He doesn't make mistakes, and that He purposes all things for the believer's benefit and His own glory. In addition to remembering these truths, the good theologian *actively* and *purposefully* applies these biblical principles as he responds to his loss. Because he knows that he has the mind of Christ, he will take every thought captive unto the Lord (1 Corinthians 2:16; 2 Corinthians 10:5). As he renews his mind by reflecting on the Cross, he will think and act as one forgiven (Luke 7:36-50; Romans 6:11; Ephesians 4:23). As he exercises biblically-based mind renewal, he will view the situation from God's perspective and grieve in a godly manner, even though he will not find the same comfort that he can with the death of a believer.

Sometimes God places believers in situations that force them to trust Him. Especially in these situations, God is removing the dross from the believer's faith, thereby sharpening his spiritual "IQ" in the areas of trust and hope (1 Corinthians 10:13; James 1:2-4; 1 Peter 1:6-7). It is all too easy for believers to consider the loss of a loved one without reflecting on the person's unbelieving attitude and lifestyle. From our perspective, it may seem that knowledge of the final destiny of the one who has died would lessen the sorrow, but sometimes, it is just not clear whether or not the person who died was saved. That was true for me when several members of my family died. If they died as unbelievers, knowing their final destiny may have increased my sorrow over their deaths. But, the truth of the matter is that I didn't need to know their final destiny in order to honor God in my sorrow. God has provided me with everything I need for life and godliness, and if I truly needed to know, God would have provided that information (2 Peter 1:3-4).

So what other thoughts should a believer think at the death of an unbeliever? First, the believer rightly acknowledges that God is perfectly just, holy, and righteous to punish those who rebel and oppose Him (2 Thessalonians 1:5-10). We know that after death there is judgment, and it is the reality of standing before the Just Judge of the earth that produces the sting of death (Hebrews 9:27; Genesis 18:25; Hebrews 2:14-15; 1 Corinthians 15:54-57). The unbeliever has to face that judgment without the possibility of pleading the blood of Christ (Hebrews 9:22). On the other hand, the believer is able to plead the shed blood of Christ as his substitute—this is the second "right thought" for the believer. It is solely by the grace and mercy of God that the believer has been judged in Christ and accepted by God as His child. The third "right thought" is that the believer grieves God's way only when he balances a right view of God's justice and holiness with a joyful and thankful respect for God's mercy and love.

Death forces the believer in a real and personal way to reflect on God's justice, holiness, goodness, and mercy, especially when a loved one dies. Focusing on the destiny of people rather than focusing on the Cross—God's justice and love—can result in a downward spiral of hopelessness, helplessness, resentment, and bitterness, all of which dishonors God. The final destiny of the unbelieving rebel is as much a demonstration of God's justice and holiness as the believer's destiny is a demonstration of God's love (Romans 9:22-23). In Christ, God demonstrated His love, mercy, and grace as well as His justice and holiness (Romans 3:21-26).

We need to train ourselves to consider spiritual *and* physical death so that we are constantly aware of the reality of the Cross, hell, and heaven. In doing so, when we are faced with the death of an unbeliever, we boldly and gently seize the moment as an evangelistic opportunity.[22] Instead of concentrating on his individual loss, the believer, and only the believer, is able to look at the Cross in a way that moves him to present Christ as the only true hope in this life and the next.

---

22   You may be wondering how to do this. Praying for wisdom and boldness in applying that wisdom certainly are excellent starting points. Seeking an opportunity to appropriately speak God's truth is a logical second step. And thirdly, coming alongside truly needy people and presenting Christ as Savior and Lord as the only answer for a truly satisfied and contented life completes the process.

CHAPTER 7

More Biblical Examples

SCRIPTURE GIVES EXAMPLES OF SAINTS who properly grieved in order to teach, encourage, and motivate you to do the same. Let's consider some of them.

David, a man after God's own heart, had his share of trouble and grief. One such episode is recorded in 1 Samuel 30.

> David and his men reached Ziklag on the third day. Now the Amalekites had raided the Negev and Ziklag. Thy had attacked Ziklag and burned it and had taken captive the women and all who were in it, both young and old. They killed none of them but carried them off as they went on their way. When David and his men came to Ziklag, they found it destroyed by fire and their wives and sons and daughters taken captive. So David and his men wept aloud until they had no strength left to weep. David's two wives had been captured – Ahinoam of Jezreel and Abigail, the widow of Nabal of Carmel. David was greatly distressed because the men were talking of stoning him; each one was bitter in spirit because of his sons and daugh-

*ters. But David found strength in the Lord. Then David said
to Abiathar, the priest, the son of Ahimelech, "Bring me the
ephod." Abiathar brought it to him, and David inquired of the
Lord, "Shall I pursue this raiding party? Will I overtake them?"
"Pursue them," he answered. "You will certainly overtake them
and succeed in rescue."*

(1 Samuel 30:1-8)

David and his men had experienced a terrible loss at the
hands of the Amalekites (verse 3). They wept aloud until they
could weep no more (verse 4). David's men threatened mutiny,
and David became greatly "distressed." The word indicates
that he was in a bind—pressure (verse 6). David could have
complicated his grief by focusing on his loss and becoming
angry and revengeful as his men did. However, "David found
strength in the Lord" (v.6). David remembered who Jehovah
was and who he himself was, and David acted upon his vi-
able, personal, and intimate relationship with Jehovah. Motivated by that relationship, he inquired of the Lord and then
proceeded to action (verse 8). What a marvelous example of
proper grieving!

Next, consider David's action in 2 Samuel 12:15-25. This
IDLS was occasioned by his sin (verses 13-14). The child
who had been born out of adultery became ill (verse 15). In
an effort to have God spare the child, David fasted, prayed,

and "mortified" himself (verses 16-17). After his servants told him that the child had died, they expected a violent reaction. Instead, David got up from the ground, washed, went into God's house, and worshipped. He refreshed himself physically and then went and comforted Bathsheba, the child's mother (verse 20-24).

These two accounts of David's response to loss are quite similar. In each case, David's grief was not complicated by self-pity, anger, or bitterness. Rather, he refreshed Himself in the Lord and ministered to others in God's name. There was no process, no journey, no denial, no bargaining with God, and no turning to some resource other than his God.

Now consider Job. In the book that bears his name, Job was described by God as blameless and upright (Job 1:1, 8; 2:3). In chapter one, Job received tragic news of marked changes in his circumstances (1:14-19). Four times in staccato fashion, Job was faced with loss:

1) Sabeans attacked and carried off the oxen and the donkeys and killed all but one servant (1:15).

2) "The fire of God" burned up the sheep and all his servants but one (1:16).

3) Chaldean raiders carried off his camels and killed all but one servant (1:17).

4) The wind struck the house that his sons and daughters were visiting, and they were killed (1:18).

His response is given in verses 20-22:

> *At this, Job got up and tore his robe and shaved his head.*
> *Then he fell to the ground in worship and said, "Naked I came*
> *from my mother's womb and naked will I depart. The Lord*
> *gave and the Lord has taken away; may the name of the Lord*
> *be praised." In all of this, Job did not sin by charging God with*
> *wrongdoing.* (Job 1:20-22)

As if by second nature, when faced with this kind of adversity, Job mourned by tearing his clothes and shaving his head. He grieved appropriately, properly, and purposefully. His primary reference was vertical—he worshipped God by prostrating himself before God and acknowledged two basic principles of life: God's fundamental ownership of all things and His providential control of every event in life. Worship in the midst of loss is always proper. At this point in his life, Job did not raise his fist against God or charge God with wrongdoing, unfaithfulness, or a failing to love (1:22). And in chapter 2, we read that Job experienced even more and greater trouble of a deeper, personal nature: his body was attacked. The pain was excruciating, and there was no relief. He received counsel from his wife to curse God and die (2:9). Her counsel was similar to what Satan predicted for Job if he was "squeezed" hard enough (1:11; 2:5).

Job responded to his wife with strong, truthful, and timely

counsel (2:10). *He replied, "You are talking like a foolish woman. Shall we accept good from God and not trouble?" In all this, Job did not sin in what he said.* His reply to his wife is much like his response to God as is recorded in chapter 1:20-22.

Clearly, his response to his dramatically and radically changed circumstances was not a journey or a process of grieving. He was a real person in a real world with terrible circumstances. He felt deeply the reality of life in a fallen world, but he responded to these devastating life changes by focusing on God. Therefore, he was able to give wise counsel to his wife in the midst of hard times.

Paul certainly faced great trouble and understood loss. What was his exhortation to the Thessalonians? "*Now we don't want you to be ignorant, brothers, about those who sleep, lest you grieve as others who have no hope*" (1 Thessalonians 4:13). These saints had faulty ideas regarding Jesus' return and consequently about those who had died prior to it. False teachers taught that no believer would die before Christ's second coming. Puzzled and grieved over the death of some of their friends and family members, the people wanted to know about those who had died and what had happened to Christ.

As Paul often did, he exhorted his readers to be correctly informed.[23] Ignorance among God's people leads to untruth and error, always dishonors God, and is bad for the believer.

---

23   Romans 1:13; 11:25; 1 Corinthians 10:1; 12:1; 2 Corinthians 1:8.

In this case, ignorance regarding the brothers and sisters who had died would lead to grieving without hope.

In the case of the Thessalonians, we have seen that Paul pointed out the universal biblical truth that grief is appropriate and proper. Godly grieving is not self-centered or complicated by such things as doubt, confusion, worry, fear, anger, or bitterness. These wrong responses will occur unless the believer evaluates his situation through the grid of God's truth. Feeling helpless and hopeless, a person may choose to cease functioning. The secular world calls this "depression." Succinctly, the biblical understanding of this feeling state is giving in to feelings, thereby giving up on responsible living. Faced with a significant loss, the believer has a choice. He will either look to God's Word or some other "help." Paul points the Thessalonians to God's Word.

The specific truth that would enable the Thessalonians to grieve with hope is given in verse 14 of chapter 4: "If we believe that Jesus died and rose again, in the same way, through Jesus, God also will bring with Him those who sleep." Paul's solution to God-dishonoring grief and grieving was focusing on the resurrection. Because Jesus died and rose, so too will the believer. Man's time is limited—it is in God's hand (Psalm 31:15). There is more *to* life than "right now," and there is more *of* life to live "right now." There is a God to glorify by embracing the joys of resurrection life now (Philippians

4:4-9; Colossians 3:1-3; 1 John 3:1-3). The resurrection is important in developing a true theology of change through loss (Romans 6:9-10). Paul spells out this truth in its entirety in 1 Corinthians 15.

Jacob is an example of grieving in a God-*dishonoring* way (Genesis 37:31-36; 42:36-38; 43:11-14; 44:33-34; 45:25-28; 47:9-10). The Bible tells us that the trickster Jacob had favorites—Rachel and Joseph (Genesis 29:30; 37:3). His display of favoritism (one example being the giving of the multicolored coat to Joseph) placed Joseph in physical jeopardy. When Jacob thought that Joseph had died, his response reflected the value he placed on his relationship with Joseph and Rachel. The Bible tells us that "he refused to be comforted" by his sons and daughters (37:35). His response was much like Aunt Joan and Aunt Sarah.

The Bible captures Jacob's pathos during the time of Joseph's absence (42:36 –43:14): he concluded that "Everything is against me" (42:36)! Functionally, Jacob had raised his fist against God. Jacob's grieving was complicated by self pity: "As for me, if I am bereaved, I am bereaved" (43:14). He was overwhelmed with life. Even so, God was gracious to Jacob, and his spirit was revived—but only when he learned that Joseph was alive physically (45:27). Jacob, the doubter, required physical evidence of Joseph before he would say, *"I'm convinced! My son Joseph is still alive. I will go up and see him before I die"*

(45:28). Seemingly, Jacob had lost sight of the living God. His grieving focused on the hardness of his life, and consequently, he made life harder for his family and himself.

Jacob's response to loss was in sharp contrast to Abraham, his grandfather (Genesis 22:1-14). The principle of resurrection life (living daily with an eternal perspective) was evident in the life of Abraham, which enabled him "to pass the test" set before him (Genesis 22:1-14). Abraham received instructions from God that he should take Isaac and sacrifice him—kill his *only* son, the son of promise (22:1-2). In obedience and without hesitation, he set out early the next day and continued on his journey for three days (22:3-4). The Bible doesn't tell us what Abraham was thinking during that time, but we know that Abraham believed in the resurrection because he believed in a faithful, promise-keeping God (Galatians 3:8-16; Hebrews 11:8-19). In Genesis 22:8, Abraham answered Isaac: *"God himself will provide the lamb for the burnt offering, my son." And the two of them went on together.* Abraham reasoned that God would raise the dead, including his only son, Isaac (Hebrews 11:19). Abraham rightly responded to the potential loss of his only son because of his view of a personal, providing God and resurrection life.

Lastly, let's look at Judas, the betrayer. Did he grieve? If so, what kind was it? Apparently, he had loved money more than he loved Christ (Matthew 26:14-15). When he realized the consequences of selling out Jesus, he was seized with remorse.[24] Properly, he went to the spiritual leaders, acknowledged his actions as wrong, and returned the money, but their cold, heartless response cut him deeply (Matthew 27:3-5). Judas still could have grieved God's way. All was not lost. Yet he chose to dishonor God by focusing on self. Scripture emphasizes Judas' feelings and his response to them; in essence, that he felt sorry for himself.[25] He had wrong thinking about himself and Christ and chose to take his own life. In his arrogance and sorrow, he attempted to do with his own blood only what Christ's shed blood accomplished for all believers. Hopelessly remorseful, Judas continued to dishonor God and reaped eternal consequences.

---

24   In the original, the word is *metameleia* which means 'sorrow afterward,' 'regret.' It is used only five times: Matthew 21:29,32; 27:3; 2 Corinthians 7:10; Hebrews 7:21

25   Suicide, the taking of one's life, was Judas' way of handling hard times and guilt. In that choice, he served self, but he was still faced with the reality of standing before God. Suicide is the ultimate "getting inside yourself" in order to flee trouble, but it fails miserably. Judas failed to seek godly men who would present God's truth gently but firmly. The best resource for anyone who may be down (the believer may be down but never out: 2 Corinthians 4:8-10) is a godly person who will open the truths of Christ and the Cross.

CHAPTER 8

Objections

I CAN HEAR IT NOW (and I have).

"That Bible stuff is OK for someone else, but not me—at least not now. My situation is just too painful."

"I just can't go on like this. I need real help and support."

"How will I ever make it? Nothing seems to be able to fill the void and loneliness. You would understand if you were in my shoes."

"Right now I am in so much distress that I need real help. I can't see Jesus, and I can't feel Him. I need to go somewhere that I can feel the warmth and care of someone who has been through the same thing and knows what it's like."

Is this how you are thinking and feeling?

These same notions were expressed by Jesus' disciples and friends. Jesus disciples' stated their desire to remain with Jesus through thick and thin; however, when hard times came and when faced with loss—even imprisonment or death—they abandoned Jesus. Their relationship with Christ and its joy did not motivate them to use the IDLS to follow their Master. Instead, they focused on themselves and their personal losses.

Scripture records two specific occasions in which those close to Jesus accused Him of not caring when they were faced with hard and uncertain times. Consider these verses: *Jesus was in the stern, sleeping on a cushion. The disciples woke him and said to him, "Teacher, don't you care if we drown?"* (Mark 4:38), and (Luke 10:40): *But Martha was distracted by all the preparations that had to be made. She came to him and asked, "Lord, don't you care that my sister has left me to do the work by myself? Tell her to help me!"* There was no doubt that in each scenario, the people were in troubling, even fearful situations. These examples show how easy it is to functionally "raise a fist" at Jesus. From our perspective, it is startling how irreverently they spoke to the Son of God. But in reality, sometimes we "raise our fist" at God, figuratively in our hearts where no one sees. We do this when we turn to other means for a salve for our wounds. But we actually make them worse when we respond in that manner. God's way is to focus on what we *do* have in Christ, depending on His truth as our source of comfort and direction rather than turning to the crumbs that fall from the secular table of human reasoning in order "to handle grief."

What *do* believers have in Christ? They have a heavenly Father; the crucified Savior; a personal and intimate relationship with the Father in Christ; the comfort and influence of the indwelling Holy Spirit; and the completed, written Word as their lamp and mirror. In that Word, God has provided a number of books and passages that comfort the believer. Consider the book of Hebrews. The author was writing to Jewish Christians who were facing great loss because of their choice to be followers of Christ. In the face of adversity, they were tempted to go back to their former way of life. In order to encourage endurance as they lived out their Christian faith, the author illustrates the benefit and necessity of living out of one's relationship to Christ. He understood the importance of that relationship for evaluating life with an eternal perspective when facing hard times. He was fully aware of the outward pressures on his congregation—Jewish Christians being ill-treated and even persecuted by non-Christian Jews. As motivation for them to remain true and endure, the Holy Spirit provided the book of Hebrews, which teaches that Jesus is better than any other alternative. Jesus and His answers for life were far superior and entirely sufficient for anything that Judaism and the culture had to offer, and the same is true for us today.

The author points specifically to how Jesus is superior even in times of trouble. Hebrews 4:15 states:

> *We don't have a high priest who isn't able to sympathize with our weaknesses, but One who has been tempted in every way that we are, yet without sin.*

The passage speaks of Christ's identification with His people and sinful humanity with its miseries and problems (the word translated "weaknesses" refers to the fallen human condition). As the God-man, Christ fully identified with mankind, but without sin. Jesus was their true Helper as well as Sympathizer. What was true for the Hebrew congregation is true for you today.

When a believer turns away from God and His wisdom, he echoes the culture's sentiment that the Cross was in vain and that God is unable to help hurting people—especially "me" right now. When faced with loss and radical change in your life, how do you respond? Do you follow Martha and the disciples' example by asking, "Do you care?" Or do you remind yourself of the fact that Christ *does* care, *does* understand, and *willingly* proved it by completing His Father's will at the cross?

CHAPTER 9

Conclusion

REFLECTING BACK ON OUR STUDY of the theology of change through loss, I encourage all believers to consider grief and grieving in light of the Word of God. Since all of life is theological, the issue before you is this: which theology will you bring to loss and change? There are many voices speaking about grief, instructing people about what grief is and how to grieve. The Bible, which is the believer's manual for life, stands out as the true beacon for you in this life.

Scripture teaches that loss is a given in God's world. Scripture teaches that grief is appropriate and proper—it should accompany loss, but in God's way. Since grieving is something that one does as a whole person, the believer needs to evaluate how to honor God with his affections, thoughts, and actions in the midst of grieving.

Grieving God's way means that the person faces the reality of the situation and understands it for what it is. Change hurts, and life can seem so overwhelming, especially when you lose a loved one. Your life is changed forever, and you face new challenges. But a believer need not complicate his grieving. Moreover, godly grieving is not a process or journey of "getting used to" or "coping with" change. The key ingredient for biblical grieving is embracing the hope which comes through biblical truth and its application.

Godly grieving recognizes that God is in the circumstances, and that He is proactive, not reactive. Scripture tells us that God is never surprised by what happens in His world, because nothing occurs outside of His decree and purpose. Therefore, the one grieving is not a victim. His loss comes from God's loving, providential hand. So, there is no reason to complicate his hurts with an exclusive self-focus. Loss hurts—it hurts you personally and often affects others. But there is a much greater hurt because a much greater Son came as the innocent Lamb of God and was impaled on the cross for sinners such as you. Loss must always point to the greater One and His hurt. When you choose to think right thoughts (established biblical truth) instead of focusing on how you feel, you put your loss into proper perspective, and you will be able grieve God's way.

Hope will focus the believer's thoughts on God and His promises. When a grieving person relies on his own understanding and focuses on his feelings, he faces the situation without hope and is therefore devoid of biblical wisdom. This will move him downward in a spiral of hopelessness, helplessness, and despair; in other words, depression.

Appropriate and proper grieving is purposeful, hopeful, and uncomplicated by bitterness, resentment, overwhelming loss, or anger (1 Thessalonians 4:13). Therefore, your tears of grief can be mixed with tears of joy. Godly grieving always has an element of joy because the believer remembers the good news of salvation: God knows, sees, and cares for His children, even in IDLS. Loss and grief *should* point you to the misery of sin and the cost of reversing its effects. Your view of your salvation and God's provision should move you to a greater awareness and understanding of God's love (Ephesians 3:14-21). In contrast to the culture's teaching on grief and grieving, change and loss should force you to reflect on what you have in Christ rather than what you have lost. This vertical focus includes the certainty of eternal life and a foretaste of heaven on this earth through the indwelling Holy Spirit and His Word. And this proper vertical focus will help you be thankful for God's past provisions and will help you joyfully anticipate God's continued provisions.

As bad as it hurts, the loss that you have experienced, even the loss of a loved one, has been providentially brought by God into your life for the purpose of growing you into Christlikeness (Romans 8:28-29). Change and loss force you to review the impact of the Cross and Jesus' ministry on your whole person—your thinking, desiring, and acting. So you are now faced with a choice: will you receive help or reject it? Receiving help from God and His people can be an encouragement for you and others in the family of God. Your loss provides a unique opportunity for you to move away from self in order to serve others even when it is hard. Service in hard times is a testimony of God's grace.

Sometimes, it is in dark, uncertain times that the ever present God is experienced most profoundly. He uses trouble in the lives of His servants for them to seek and find Him and His comfort (2 Corinthians 1:3-4, 8-10). When that help is found, the believer will be able to show others the same help that he received as he comforts them (Job 42:7-10; 2 Corinthians 1:3-10). God will never leave His people. His love is wide, deep, long, and high, such that it encircles and strengthens the believer in any and every circumstance (Ephesians 3:14-21). It is to your advantage, believer, to grieve His way and for His glory. May God bless you as you do, always remembering Paul's words.

No, in all these things we are more than conquerors through him who loved us. For I am convinced that neither death nor life, neither angels nor demons, neither the present nor the future, nor any powers, neither height nor depth, nor anything else in all creation, will be able to separate us from the love of God that is in Christ Jesus our Lord.

(Romans 8:35–37)

CHAPTER 10

Homework Assignments

THESE QUESTIONS ARE TO ASSIST you in grieving God's way. Please answer them on a separate sheet of paper. These assignments can form the basis for a Bible study or your own personal study. The answers can be reviewed with one of your church leaders.

1. List the changes that you are experiencing or have experienced, beginning with the immediate loss.

2. Record how those changes are unpleasant and the reasons why.

3. Summarize the pleasant aspects and benefits of your previous situation.

4. Record the source of those benefits.

5. According to 1 Thessalonians 5:18, Ephesians 5:20, and Romans 8:28-29, what is a proper response to your loss and why?

6. In what ways are you to express thankfulness for the benefits of that situation?

7. When you focus inordinately on your loss, what happens?

8. What should be a proper focus now? See Philippians 3:3-11.

9. According to 2 Corinthians 1:3-11, when your attention is on the God of blessings, what should you think and do?

10. What does it mean to be comforted by God? In what ways have you received comfort, and what has been the result?

11. How and in what ways have you been served by others during this time? Out of joyful thankfulness, who can you serve and how?

12. What questions do you have that you need help in answering?

Appendix A: *lupeo* and *lupe*

THE WORDS *LUPEO/LUPE* GENERALLY MEAN
"to afflict with sorrow" and "sadness." In the New Testament, these two words are the most commonly used ones
to translate the word "grief." In fact, the Septuagint (the
most important Greek translation of the Old Testament)
translates thirteen different Hebrew verbs by *lupeo*. In the
New Testament, the noun occurs some sixteen times and
the verb, twenty-six times. Therefore, attention should
be given to these words in order to develop a theology
of loss through grief.

The Gospel of Matthew (six occasions)

14:9: *"The king (Herod) was <u>upset</u> but because of his oaths and
those who sat with him at the table, he commanded them to give it
to her."*

The word for grief is translated "upset." It is an example of
"inner-man turmoil" that developed when Herod was faced

with doing something ungodly (killing John the Baptist) or appearing as a liar and one who doesn't keep vows before his friends.

17:23: *"who will kill Him, but on the third day He will be raised. And the disciples became terribly <u>upset</u>."*

Upon hearing Jesus' prediction of His death, the disciples responded in grief.

18:31: *When his fellow slaves saw what had happened, they were greatly <u>upset</u> and went and told their lord all about what had taken place.*

The servants were grieved by the man who had been forgiven infinitely and yet failed to forgive his fellow servant.

19:22: *But hearing that statement, the young man left <u>sadly</u> because he had many possessions.*

The rich young ruler was faced with a choice much like King Herod in Matthew 14:9. He opted for that which he treasured.

26:22, 37: *They became terribly <u>upset,</u> and each one began to say to Him, "It isn't I, is it, Lord?" He took Peter and the two sons of Zebedee and He became <u>sad</u> and distressed.*

Apparently the disciples were struck with amazement, and perhaps guilt, at the fact that Jesus considered one of them His betrayer.

The Gospel of Mark (two occasions)

10:22: *But gloom spread over his face at that statement, and he* *went away* <u>*upset*</u> *(this was because he had great possessions).*

See Matthew 18:31.

14:19: *They began to get* <u>*upset*</u> *and one after another said to Him, "It isn't I, is it?"*

See Matthew 26:22, 27.

The Gospel of Luke (one occasion)

22:45: *When He rose from prayer and went to His disciples, He found them asleep, worn out by* <u>*sorrow.*</u>

Grief, unrestrained, can deplete one of energy. See 1 Samuel 30:1-8.

The Gospel of John (six occasions)

16:6: *Rather, because I have spoken these things, your hearts are filled with* <u>*pain*</u>.

Jesus was continuing His theology class the night before He died. In verse 1, He gave the reason for what follows: so you won't stumble and fall into sin. Jesus predicted their suffering and persecution (verse 2-3). In verse 4, He reiterates why he has spoken these things, thereby explaining verse 1 and His view of stumbling. They are to remember what He is saying to them. In verse 5, He explains His departure but adds that no one has asked Him His destination. They are grieved at His words rather than being comforted and joyful.

16:20: *Let me assure you that you will weep and moan while the world will rejoice. You will be* <u>*pained*</u>, *but your* <u>*pain*</u> *will turn to joy.*

16:21: *When a woman is giving birth, she has <u>pain</u> because her time has come, but when she delivers the child she doesn't remember her trouble because of the joy that a child has been born into the world.*

16:22: *So then, you too will have <u>pain</u> at this time, but I will see you again and your hearts will rejoice, and nobody will take your joy from you.*

In these three verses, Jesus pointed to the reality of pain, misery, sorrow, and grief in the present world, especially for believers. But their anguish, like His, was to be temporary and finite but purposeful.

21:17: *He said to him a third time, "Simon, son of John, do you care for me?" Peter was deeply <u>hurt</u> that He said to him the third time, "Do you care for Me?" He said to Him, "Lord you know everything; You know that I care for you." Jesus said to him, "Feed My sheep."*

Peter was upset at Jesus' questions, even though he had answered Jesus using a different word than Jesus had used (Jesus had used *agapeo* in His first two questions (v.15-16), and Peter responded using *phileo*). Then Jesus used Peter's own word when He asked a third time if Peter loved/cared for Him. Apparently, Peter was cut to the core and was deeply hurt. Peter did profess His devotion to Christ, who reinstated Peter.

The writings of Paul (twenty occasions)

Romans 9:2: *that I have great <u>pain</u> and continual anguish in* *my heart.*

Paul grieved over Israel's rebellion against God.

2 Corinthians 2

v.1: *But I made up my mind not to pay you another <u>painful</u> visit.*

v.2: *If I cause you <u>pain,</u> who will be there to make me happy except the same ones that I caused <u>pain</u>?*

v.3: *So I wrote what I did for fear that when I came I might be caused <u>pain</u> by the very persons who ought to make me glad. I am confident about all of you that what makes me glad, makes you glad.*

v.4: *It was out of much affliction and anguish of heart and through many tears that I wrote to you, not to cause you <u>pain</u>, but rather, to let you know the fullness of love that I have for you.*

v.5: *But if somebody has caused <u>pain</u>, he hasn't caused <u>pain</u> to me, but to some extent − I don't want to put it too strongly − to all of you.*

v.6: *The punishment that the majority inflicted on this person is sufficient.*

v.7: *so instead of going on with that, you should rather forgive and help him so that he won't be overwhelmed by too much <u>pain</u>.*

Paul is referring to the hard work of his pastoral activities in regards to the Corinthians. The work has been painful, but it was an act of love (v.4). The call to repentance can be a time of sorrow and grieving, both for Paul and the congregation. The fruit of those labors has been repentance, both from the congregation and the incestuous man. He is now ready to be restored (v.5–11). It is time to turn pain to joy, and Paul outlined how to do that in verses 7–8.

6:10: *as deeply <u>pained</u> but always rejoicing, as poor but making many rich, as having nothing but possessing everything.*

Beginning in verse 4, Paul had begun to list the hardships in his life as a way of recommending himself to the Corinthians. He did so in order to remove any stumbling block to the preaching of the gospel. So intent was he on furthering the gospel, he determined never to discredit his ministry (verse 3).

7:8: *Even if I caused you <u>pain</u> by my letter, I am not sorry for it (though indeed I was sorry). I see that you were caused <u>pain</u> by that letter for a short time.*

7:9: *but I am now delighted – not that you were <u>pained</u> but that your <u>pain</u> led to repentance. You were caused <u>pain</u> by God that you might in no way suffer loss by us.*

7:10: *<u>Pain</u> that comes from God produces a repentance leading to salvation that no one needs to be sorry about. But <u>pain</u> that comes from the world produces death.*

7:11: *Now just look at the earnestness that this <u>pain</u> from God has produced in you; what a desire to defend yourselves, what indignation, what fear, what longing, what enthusiasm, what concern for justice! In every way you have proved yourselves to be innocent in the issue.*

These verses contrast godly, life-changing repentance and worldly sorrow. The Corinthians responded in the way that they did because Paul's letter moved them to true repentance. Their pain came from God, and therefore, it was not self-focused. As a proof for that, they repented and eventually showed fruits of that repentance. Paul focused on their response to his letter—their repentance and its fruit—rather than his own sorrow, thereby enabling him to glory in the good that pain rightly handled brings. In this case, the good was true repentance.

Romans 14:15: *Now if you are <u>hurting</u> your brother because of food, you are no longer walking by love. Don't let your food ruin a person for whom Christ died.*

Christians can be the source of pain and misery for a brother or sister in the Lord. Differences of opinion are never to be used to discriminate or divide God's people.

Ephesians 4:30: *And don't <u>grieve</u> God's Holy Spirit with whom you were sealed for the redemption day.*

This is the only place in Scripture that speaks of grieving the Holy Spirit, and it occurs in the context of unity of the body of Christ and the place of godly communication in promoting and maintaining that unity.

Philippians 2:27 (Jay Adam's Christian Counselor's New Testament): *Indeed he was sick and came near to death, but God had mercy on him (not on him only, but also on me, less I* *should have <u>grief</u> upon <u>grief</u>!).*

Paul is speaking of his companion Epaphroditus, who had been ill. Paul appreciated him as God's gift to Paul, who was appropriately pained at Epaphroditus's sickness.

1 Thessalonians 4:13: *Now, we don't want you to ignorant, brothers, about those who sleep, lest you <u>grieve</u> as others who have no hope.*

See section VIII for a thorough explanation of this verse.

Non-Pauline epistles (three occasions)

Hebrews 12:11: *Of course all discipline seems <u>painful</u> rather than pleasant for the moment, but later on it yields the peaceful fruit of righteousness to those who have been trained by it.*

Verses 5–11 refer to God's corrective intervention (discipline) in the believer's life that is painful but is purposeful. It is also a sign of membership in God's family.

1 Peter 1:6: *You should be glad about this even if now you may have to be <u>sad</u> because of many kinds of trials.*

Hard times are purposeful and when responded to God's way will be beneficial for the believer.

1 Peter 2:19: *One finds favor if out of conscience toward God he bears up under <u>pain</u> when suffering unjustly.*

This speaks of affliction from the outside. In this case, Peter was referring to Roman persecutions. Physical afflictions are part of the hard times of trials.

Appendix B: *KLAIO*

THE WORD *KLAIO* IS USED some forty times and is translated as "weep, wept, weeping" and "to cry, mourn, and wail." It indicates not only the shedding of tears but also the physical and external expression of grief. It can mean any loud expression of grief such as "to lament." It is used in a variety of ways.

I. **It describes man's reaction to death.**

    A. **Mark 5:38-39 (Luke 8:49-56):** These verses give a picture of the mourning customs of the Eastern culture surrounding the death of the synagogue ruler's daughter. The people were <u>weeping</u>.

    B. **Mark 16:10**: Verses 9-20 are omitted in earlier manuscripts. Verse 10 reported Mary Magdalene <u>weeping</u> in front of Jesus' disciples.

    C. **Luke 7:13**: Before Jesus raised the widow of Nain's son, He told her not to <u>cry</u>.

    D. **Luke 8:52 (Mark 5:38-30)**: Jesus was at Jarius' house, a synagogue leader whose daughter had died. The people were weeping and <u>crying</u> and wailing.

E. **John 11:31**: Mary was <u>mourning</u> at the death of her brother Lazarus.

F. **John 20:11, 13**: These verses described the conversation between Mary Magdalene and angels, and Jesus' question to her, post-resurrection.

G. **Acts 9:39:** A number of the widows <u>wept</u> at Dorcas' death.

II. **It expresses the violence of grief**.

In the Old Testament, the whole person responded to loss. It expressed dependence on God. In the New Testament, grief was expressed violently.

A. **Acts 21:13**: Upon Paul's departure to Jerusalem, he asked his friends why they were <u>crying</u> and "breaking my heart" (the word is used only here in the New Testament and it means "to crush a spirit").

B. **Philippians 3:18**: Paul <u>wept</u> as he was thinking of those who lived as enemies of Christ.

C. **Mark 5:38–39; Luke 7:13; John 11:31, 33; Acts 9:39** (see above).

D. **Romans 12:15; 1 Corinthians 7:30**: These verses refer to one's response when being face to face with affliction.

III. **It should be man's reaction to sin.**

A. **Matthew 26:75; Mark 14:72; Luke 22:62**: These passages record Peter's response to his own rejection of Christ.

B. **Luke 6:21**: see under the appropriateness of weeping

C. **James 4:9**: verses 6-10 are a clear exhortation to repentance. Grief is a vital part of repentance.

IV. **It expresses the appropriateness of grief.**

A. **Luke 6:21**: Jesus taught on the ways to happiness. One way was to weep, which meant to repent because the object of one's weeping was offense of a holy and loving God. Repentance was the gospel message of John and Jesus, and to date the nation of Israel had forsaken that call. Repentance now would lead to laughing—joy in due time.

B. **Luke 7:32 (Matthew 11:17)**: Jesus asked in verse 31, to what should He compare the people of the present generation. He gave the answer in verse 32: they rejected John (they didn't dance at the playing of the flute—no joy), and they rejected Christ (they didn't cry; they didn't grieve). In response to both Himself and John, the people were sinfully inappropriate.

C. **Luke 7:38**: Those who truly appreciate the magnitude of God's forgiveness often express their gratitude and dependence on God by weeping and mourning

(Matthew 5:4). True repentance is a characteristic of those in God's kingdom and expresses spiritual maturity.

D. **Luke 19:41; 23:28**: Jesus wept over Jerusalem, and He told the women not to make Him the object of their weeping. He told them to follow His example and weep for themselves and their children.

E. **John 20:13, 15:** Mary Magdalene was weeping, believing that death had won the victory. She wept and grieved without hope (1 Thessalonians 4:13). Jesus told her that this was not the time to grieve, especially in a God-dishonoring manner.

F. **James 4:9:** Repentance is a time of weeping and mourning.

G. **James 5:1**: Those with material riches must understand and act upon the fact that the material and temporal are finite. When riches and things are raised to a level of competition with their allegiance to God, distresses will come on them (Luke 16:14, 19-31; 1 Timothy 6:1-10). Rather than seek to serve possessions and things, they must repent and turn from idols to serve the living God (1 Thessalonians 1:9).

H. **Revelation 5:5**: One of the elders told John not to weep. Why? Jesus, the Lamb, is the Lion who has defeated the enemy. He is King of kings and Lord of history. He would open the scroll. It wasn't time to mourn but to focus on Him and His words.

V. **It expresses the object of one's grief.**

A. **Luke 23:28**: Jesus exhorted the women to change their focus of grief. They did not understand the magnitude of their sin, God's justice, God's wrath, God's love, their inability, and the greatness of Him, the Messiah. Therefore, their grief was ill-founded and did not move toward any useful purpose.

VI. **New Testament passages in the Gospels and Epistles**

A. **The Gospel of Matthew** (two occasions)

1. **Matthew 2:18**: Matthew quotes Jeremiah in response to Herod's decree to murder all boys less than two years of age. Grief was appropriate.

2. **Matthew 26:75/Mark 14:72**: Peter was consciously aware of his sin in his whole person, as was Mary Magdalene in Luke 7:38. Therefore, weeping is expressed as one acknowledges and agrees with God's assessment of him and his thoughts and actions.

B. **The Gospel of Mark** (four occasions)

1. **Mark 5:38-39 (Luke 8:49-56):** The people were crying loudly at the death of Jarius' daughter.

2. **Mark 16:10**: This verse is found only in later

manuscripts.

3. **Mark 14:72** (see Matthew 26:75)

C. **The Gospel of Luke (**thirteen occasions)

  1. **Luke 6:21**: Happy/blessed are those who <u>weep</u>. In Luke, Jesus taught the road to happiness came first from what people are (Matthew 5:3 and Luke 6:20): poor in their own spirit of importance and achievement. They have nothing except their own sinfulness to offer God. Those poor in spirit will mourn (repent) over their own sins.

  2. **Luke 6:25**: Woe to you who laugh now, for you will mourn and weep. The tables will be turned. The rich in their own spirit lived self-focused and enjoyed the wrong things. Their presumed joy was only a prelude to weeping.

  3. **Luke 7:13**: The compassionate Jesus told the widow of Nain not to cry.

  4. **Luke 7:32**: Jesus critiques the Pharisees, saying they are like children not willing to play the game that was assigned and most appropriate to play. Playing the flute (Jesus' ministry) represented a joyful game, and John the Baptist's ministry (funeral dirge) represented a mournful game.

  5. **Luke 7:38**: Mary Magdalene washes Jesus' feet out of sheer gratitude and amazement.

6. **Luke 8:52**:The daughter of Jarius, the synagogue leader, had died, and the people were weeping over her death.

7. **Luke 19:41**: Jesus saw Jerusalem and wept over it.

8. **Luke 22:62**: Peter is denying Christ. Please see the parallel passages: Matthew 26:75; Mark 14:72.

9. **Luke 23:28**: Jesus told the women not to weep over Him but for themselves and their children. Jesus addressed the object of grief.

10. **Acts 9:39**:Weeping was the widows' response to Dorcas' death.

11. **Acts 21:13**:As his friends tried to dissuade Paul, he asked why they were weeping and breaking his heart.

D. **The Gospel of John and the book of Revelation** (fourteen occasions)

1. **John 11:31**:The friends assumed Mary was going off to weep.

2. **John 11:33**: Jesus saw Mary and her friends' weeping in response to Lazarus' death. He was deeply moved, troubled, agitated, and stirred up within (John 11:33; 12:27; 13:21; 14:1, 27). Grief was appropriate.

3. **John 16:20**: Jesus told the disciples that they will

weep and mourn while the world rejoices. However, this will soon be reversed.

4. **John 20:11**: Mary Magdalene was weeping outside the tomb without hope.

5. **John 20:13**: The angels asked her why she was crying.

6. **John 20:15**: Jesus asked her why she was crying.

7. **Revelation 5:4, 5**: One of the elders spoke to John and told him not to weep. At this time, grief was not appropriate.

8. **Revelation 18:9, 11, 15, 19**: Weeping was the response of the merchants at Babylon's downfall. This weeping was inappropriate in its object and its motivation.

E. **The writings of Paul** (four occasions)

1. **Romans 12:15**: Twice Paul calls for rejoicing and weeping with those who are rejoicing and weeping. This passage emphasizes the appropriateness of grief and the balance with joy.

2. **1 Corinthians 7:30**: Tough times are coming (Roman persecutions), so time is short, and everything will be in disarray.

3. **Philippians 3:18**: With tears/grief, Paul speaks of the enemies of the cross. Their activity is a burden to them (their end is destruction, verse 19),

and it is a burden to the people who receive their false teaching.

F. **The book of James** (two occasions)

   1. **James 4:9:** "Grieve, mourn, and wail. Change your laughter to mourning and your joy to gloom." James may be recalling Jesus' words of Luke 6:21. James emphasized the appropriateness of grief.

   2. **James 5:1:** There is a proper response for rich people—weep. James continues to emphasize the appropriateness of grief.

Appendix C: Additional Terms

I. *Dakruo*: It means "to shed tears." The word usually refers to the physical act of crying.

   A. **John 11:35** records one of the two instance that the word refers to Jesus' action. The other is Hebrews 5:7. Rather, Jesus is the Master of every situation. Moreover, the word *klaio* is used of Jesus only in Luke 19:41.

   B. At the death of Lazarus, Jesus simply shed a tear (**11:35**), but for unrepentant Jerusalem He grieved (see section III for a discussion of this Luke passage), rejected as Savior.

II. *Threneo*: It is a formal lamentation or a lament in audible fashion. It is also translated as *bewail*.

   A. **Matthew 11:17; Luke 7:32**: These verses refer to the Pharisees.

   B. **Luke 23:27**: This verse refers to the mourning and wailing women as they viewed Jesus carrying His cross.

C. **John 16:20**: This verse refers to the disciples.

III. *Alalazo*: This means "to make a loud sound as in a battle cry." It is a loud shouting cry and even an invocation to the gods.

A. **Mark 5:38**: It describes the scene at synagogue ruler's house.

B. **1 Corinthians 13:1**: Paul uses the word to describe a disagreeable sound or gong.

IV. *Stenazo*: The word means to groan or sigh; its root word *stenos* means narrow and contracted as when squeezed or pressed by circumstances. It is used in a general sense of sighing as an expression of inward emotion. The word *stenochoria* refers to a narrow space and territory as if one is in tight quarters. It refers to distress which arises from within, usually in the context of trouble: Romans 2:9; 8:35; 2 Corinthians 6:4; 12:10.

A. **Romans 8:23**: The creation groans awaiting the bodily redemption of believers.

B. **2 Corinthians 5:2, 4**: Paul groans when he considers the unnatural condition of a bodiless soul.

C. **Hebrews 13:17**: The congregation is to obey the elders so the elders will not groan as if shepherding was a burden.

D. **James 5:9**: James warns brothers and sisters that groaning against each other will incur God's judgment.

   E. **Mark 7:34**: The verse described Jesus' inner person as He looked up at heaven when He healed the deaf man.

V. *Kopto*: The word means to strike or beat one's breast or body. It usual indicates a loud expression of grief.

   A. **Matthew 11:17; 21:8; 24:30**

   B. **Mark 11:8**

   C. **Luke 18:13; 23:27, 48**;

   D. **Revelation 1:7; 18:9.**

VI. *Pentheo*: The word means to mourn and lament but not necessarily with an outward expression of that grief. Paul and James use it to mean an attitude of the mind with an emphasis on godly sorrow and repentance.

   A. **2 Corinthians 12:21**

   B. **Mark 16:10**

   C. **Matthew 5:4; 9:15**

   D. **1 Corinthians 5:2:** Paul called the Corinthians "arrogant" because they failed to repent, to confront their brother, and to practice church discipline.

   E. **Luke 6:25**

   F. **James 4:9**

   G. **Rev 18:11, 15, 19; 21:4**: In chapter 21, the eschatological hope is no more misery or grief —shalom.

Appendix D: Critique

CRITIQUE OF *GOD'S HEALING FOR Life's Losses*
by Robert W. Kellemen, PhD. This critique is based on
a thousand word summary of the book, also written by
the author, published online at http://www.rpmministries.
org/2010/07/a-biblical-model-of-grieving/.

The author begins his summary with an exciting statement:
"How do we face suffering face to face with God rather that
turning our backs on God..." However, he ends the sentence
with psychologically-laced terms "...during the grieving process?" His next sentence also includes psychological jargon.
"What does the journey with God look like as we find hope
when we're hurting?" Did you see it?

He then tells us that we have two basic options *for finding
God's healing* for life's losses. We can turn to the world's way.
Or, we can follow the way of God's Word.

I take exception to the emphasis placed on a healing process. The term *healing* is a pregnant, feeling-directed, and

psychologically-based term. As a physician and counselor, I am face-to-face with persons who desire healing (good feelings) rather than relying on God's grace to use unpleasant situations to become more like Christ.

Dr. Kellemen then takes the Kubler-Ross Five Stage Model of grieving and calls it "evidence-based." However, Dr. Elisabeth Kubler-Ross did not profess to be a believer and did not take the patient's relationship with the Christ into consideration as she observed dying patients. Her conclusions must be reinterpreted by biblical truth; while the unbeliever can discover facts about life, he can never uncover revealed truth and will always distort to some degree the facts that he discovers. The reason for the latter is this: no fact is neutral or uninformed and always testifies to the God of this universe. To the degree that the unbeliever separates facts from the Creator (which he will always do) he distorts God's truth. (Unfortunately, believers often follow suit, especially in the areas of the so-called hard and soft sciences.) We must ask—does the Bible demonstrate grieving as a process and a journey? I think not, and my book addresses these questions from a biblical perspective.

The author goes on to say that Dr. Kubler-Ross' stages of grief seeks to track typical grief responses in the grief process. That sentence alone tells us that he has accepted the non-biblical premise of a "grief process." In my book, I seek to affirm biblical teaching regarding grief and grieving. It seems that Kellemen assumes that "what is best to occur" comes from a fallen world's research. He contrasts what typically occurs with what he believes should occur. He then explains that he will focus on a revelation-based model that he calls "Biblical Sufferology"—what he considers to be a scripturally wise and practically relevant understanding of suffering. However, what he does is "Christianize" and "biblicize" the stages of grief, which he increases to eight. This approach relies on Kellemen's experience as a directive in writing the book. That is always potentially dangerous. Experience may color God's Word rather than God's Word coloring the interpretative grid for experience.

At the end of the summary, Kellemen asks "what is your initial response to this eight-stage biblical approach compared to the typical five-stage approach of the world?" My response is the book here in your hands.

For more information about
Dr. Jim Halla
&

Joy in Grief
please visit:

www.JimHalla.com
JimHalla@gmail.com
facebook.com/JimHalla

For more information about
AMBASSADOR INTERNATIONAL
please visit:

www.ambassador-international.com
@AmbassadorIntl
www.facebook.com/AmbassadorIntl

JOY IN GRIEF